INNER CITY HOOPS

A HISTORY OF CHICAGO BASKETBALL

BY CALVIN DAVIS

Outskirts Press, Inc.
Denver, Colorado

Inner City Hoops
A History of Chicago Basketball

Outskirts Press
http://www.outskirtspress.com

ISBN-10: 1-4327-0038-3
ISBN-13: 978-1-4327-0038-6

Outskirts Press and the "OP" logo are trademarks belonging to Outskirts Press, Inc.

Printed in the United States of America

ACKNOWLEDGEMENTS

It is very meaningful to acknowledge all of the people who have helped me along my way. I feel that many people have contributed to my development as a professional, and as a person. All of my successes are because of people who I have soaked up knowledge, and gained experiences from. Some of you may not know that I learned from you, but I've always preferred to listen rather than talk. Therefore I learned a great deal from the many conversations I've been a part of. Upon becoming director of the citywide sports program, that has changed a great deal because I am required to talk all of the time now. I really don't prefer that, but a boss has to be very verbal. Let me take this opportunity to thank all of you, and if I miss someone, I certainly did not intend to. I know I missed a few great athletes from the city also, but I believe I've listed 90% of the best individuals since the 1930's. Let me thank some people who are very special to me. First of all I'd like to thank my family for making my home warm, and peaceful. Without family love and support, I feel you have nothing. I'd especially like to thank my wife Sylvia, and my son Calvin Jr. for putting up with me and my obsession with perfection. I thank my older brother Clyde Jr., for being so well respected that I never had a problem in the neighborhood. Many people called me Little Clyde. I was very fortunate to be able to concentrate my energies on schoolwork and basketball. My seventh grade teacher, Virginia Johnson, who told my mom that I would be something special in my adult life. My grade school coaches Charles Frazier and Michael Clark for exposing me to organized basketball. My high school coaches Jim Foreman, and the late Charlie Gant and Ray Price, the best fundamental instructors I ever had at any level. Fred Holman, and Leon Richardson from William Penn University in Oskaloosa, Iowa for giving me a scholarship opportunity at Penn. Finally, I'd like to thank all of the people who have talked basketball history with me, and indirectly have contributed to my research: Bill Saxton, Landon "Sonny" Cox, George Stanton, Mark Lowry, Dr. Larry Hawkins, Jim Foreman, Louie James, Bob "Quick" Watkins, Rich "Pep" Morgan, Paul Vinson, Aaron and Glenn Willoughby, and Johnny Selvie.

I most certainly have to thank my mother Annette Davis, and my Father, the late Clyde Davis Sr. who during their 50 plus year marriage reared me in such a way that I have been able to avoid the many inner city pitfalls that plague the city neighborhoods, and breeds crime, drugs, and violence. I have seen all of these things occur right before me during my developmental years. For example, I once saw a man shot as I stood a few feet away from my family residence. That is just *one of the many* very scary, and life threatening things I've been very close to. I am an example that education and perseverance will take you above the evil forces that so many inner city youths are susceptible to. I am very thankful for my parents, because only god knows where I would be without them. I cannot say that any man other than my Dad Clyde Jay Davis Sr. was a father figure to me. I was very fortunate to have a father who worked hard, brought all of his earnings home, and took care of his family by preaching as well as practicing the right moral values. He took pride in owning his own home after retiring as a postal worker. I wish I was smart enough to keep that house which is worth 500k today. I also have the best Mom that anyone could have. There's no better housewife, or nicer person in the world as far as I'm concerned. She's was always there to support her husband for 50 years, and is presently still here to support all seven of us (her kids) no matter what the situation.

I would be remiss if I did not mention my mentors who inspired me to further my education, and seek positions where I could not only give back to the community, but have an influence on how the entire city's population of students is served. My supreme mentors beyond my mom and dad and my coaches are surprisingly to many, two women.

These two women that I'm about to mention are very

special to me, and are definitely two of my favorite ladies of all time outside of my wife. Through their mentorship, they reinforced into me the old adage, and the fact that if you work hard, good things will happen for you. My two outstanding mentors are Dr. Grace G. Dawson, and Ms. Lula M. Ford. Both of them brought me along, and mentored me when they were my principals. Grace was my first principal/mentor, and was followed by Lula who became principal at Beethoven Elementary after Grace. They looked out for me, challenged me, and inspired me to pursue education beyond a Bachelor of Arts Degree. They were right, and I'm glad I listened to their wise advice. As I look back, I am pleased that I was not afraid to put in the hard work. The rewards have been well worth the work. I can honestly say that the old saying that hard work pays off is true. I can still call those two women whenever I need some good advice or assistance. Grace had the vision twenty years ago to see that school principals in Chicago would be making more than 100, 000 dollars today, approximately 40,000 more than principals were making then. That inspired me to pursue those credentials along with the fact that in the position of principal, I could make a difference for teachers and students. She was absolutely correct. Lula, who is the Commerce Commissioner for the State of Illinois in the office of State Senate Minority Leader, the Honorable Emil Jones says: "What good is a friend in a high place if they can't help you." One of her questions to me when I was a young teacher that really made me think and plan was "What are your aspirations"? She has always helped everyone that she can. That has inspired me to do the same as much as possible. I most certainly have to mention my graduate school college professor Clarence Fitch who saw something in me, and said things that inspired me to be the best that I could be. You never know what a positive impact words can have when they are expressed in a positive way.

I must thank the following individuals for their contributions to this project:

The Chicago Sun-Times and prep sports writer Tina Akouris for helping me get to reprint the article "City Athletics Headed in Right Direction"; Tony Brooks, the author of the "Boys to Men" article that he allowed me to publish here; Robert Pruter, the author of "Early Phillips Teams" which I took excerpts from; and to Steve Tucker of the Sun-Times, my favorite Prep writer in Chicago.

TABLE OF CONTENTS

CHAPTER 1

INNER CITY HOOPS FOREWORD

You are about to read "Inner City Hoops," a history of Chicago basketball. After reading it you will come to realize that beyond a shadow of a doubt, the players in the city of Chicago play the best basketball in the world. In this book, Get ready to explore the evolution of some of Chicago's most famous players and teams. I will take you on a tour of the neighborhoods and communities around Chicago where many of these players developed their talents as "play ground ball players" on the way to becoming some of the nations most skilled professional athletes. Neighborhood tournaments which began as grass roots entertainment projects in the city grew into happenings that are among the most recognized tournaments around the country. Many of the tournaments in the Chicago area have served as excellent avenues for coaches, sports agents, and college scouts from all over the country. The leagues in the city have been used as a recruiting base for European league teams as well. Talent evaluators from all entities have visited Chicago inner city hoop sites to see well known players perform, or to recruit new players. During the summer, basketball players have a great opportunity to impress coaches and scouts while developing their games. Often times scouts will show up to observe one player, and wind up discovering another who they had no previous knowledge of. All of these basketball events began taking place on the inner city hoop scene long before AAU Tournaments. Basketball events have continuously created an opportunity for athletes from different Chicago area neighborhoods to develop relationships and mutual respect for each other. Athletes from all of the neighborhoods around the city have been able to come together and put on displays of some of the most entertaining and exciting basketball competition imaginable. I will examine how positive community spirit has evolved through basketball, including how competitive meetings on the court over the years have developed into relationships and friendships that last a lifetime. In addition, this book will give you a brief look at Chicago's most influential coaches, while discussing the talents of their players and teams. I will also discuss the successes they had in competitive play. Additionally, you will be able to visualize how many young men grew and matured into adult men through their involvement in basketball, and now have a positive impact on society as up-standing, productive citizens.

Chicago Inner City Hoops is not only about basketball, it's about diverse neighborhoods that come together for a common cause the love of the game. It covers the complexity of the development and the discovery of players, how good teams were assembled, the art of coaching diverse players, and how individuals worked toward the ultimate goal of a scholarship to college and a professional basketball career. Differences in race, culture and community borders are eliminated as players come together to play basketball. People come from all over the city (and country) to visit these tournaments just to see the best players come together to compete. The best players do not always make it to the professional status, but these people, through their involvement with playground basketball have earned local respect as being one of Chicago's greatest players. They are also viewed with a celebrity-type status in their own neighborhoods (Legends). We expect this book to be exceptionally popular in the Chicago area, as well as to basketball junkies across the country. It is a great example of how basketball steers individuals toward mental, physical, social, and emotional maturity, while teaching valuable lessons about life in general.

We hope you enjoy reading this history of Chicago basketball. As much as I enjoyed writing it and taking a look back at old fashioned neighborhood hoops. This book is for everyone who loves basketball. My hope is that young basketball enthusiasts are encouraged to read it because it is history. There may be something for all basketball lovers to learn about basketball history in the city of Chicago. It is a very positive thing for young student-athletes to learn about the history of the game, as well as the opportunities it has provided over the years. I am a living example of an inner city kid who made the most of his scholarship opportunity, and turned it into a professional career. I am very proud of the fact that I listened to my parents and followed the path of success. As Director of the Chicago Public Schools Citywide Sports Programs for our 600 plus schools, I am continuously having an impact on the lives of many young people. As I oversee the program, my hope is that the participating student-athletes will take advantage of the opportunities that are available to them through sports and education. It is a fact that many of our students absolutely do take advantage of the life changing opportunities. Of course I believe that sports is education, because the lessons you learn in sports last a lifetime.

CHAPTER 2

INNER CITY HOOPS INTRODUCTION

As we talk about Chicago Basketball, let's go back to where it all began. The playgrounds would have to be the place where most players learned to play a different, but effective version of basketball. It could be referred to as "Playground Ball". Next, we have to look at the schools where the lightweights (under 5'9" Chicago Public high school league) and heavyweights (over 5'9" Chicago Public high school league) battled for supremacy in the city, while learning the fundamentals of basketball. The YMCA's and Boy's Clubs around the city were also places where basketball skills were honed to perfection. In the fifties more media began to focus on the teams, and city basketball players began to get lots of attention. This was during the time before the first black player was allowed to perform in the NBA. Young hoopers who read this will not recognize many of the names mentioned, but these are the players who made the way for you. As you learn about my version of the basketball history of the city of Chicago, you will realize that you are standing on the shoulders of many, many great players who never made it to the NBA, but broke the ice and made inroads that contributed to the opportunities that are available today. Long before Summer Evaluation Camps, Cable TV, AAU, and Talent Scouts became part a of the basketball mix, skills were developed and players became players in the Playgrounds, Parks, and YMCA's of Chicago. As the years went by, basketball became more popular. This caused it to become more interesting, more publicized, more competitive, and more financially rewarding. All of this happened before the Michael Jordan Phenomena, which kicked off a basketball craze of its own in the city during the 80's. Basketball has also built many, many bridges across the city of Chicago, the country, and the world. As you read, you will find that there have been more NBA players from the Chicago Public League than any other city's high school league. It is an unwritten rule that city ball players are not to be included in gang activity, or crime of any kind. That is why it hurts the entire basketball fraternity when a young talented player becomes a victim of city violence, as they occasionally have. An example of the point I'm trying to make is the case of Ben Wilson, the Simeon High School star who was ranked the number one high school player in the country prior to being slain while visiting the neighborhood school store.

He was shot after an altercation with a local resident. Players are normally recognized above the crowd, and respected as well as protected by neighborhood and city residents. How could you not recognize and respect the 6'8" starting center from the defending state champion Simeon Wolverines, your neighborhood school? This is a perfect depiction of a senseless shooting, as well as a waste of a life with so much potential. I refer to this very well publicized and very tragic incident to highlight the fact that Basketball, in the city of Chicago, for the most part, breaks down barriers that exist between different neighborhoods, and different gang factions. This was a rare and random exception where the respect for athletes in the community that always applies did not apply in this random case. With the exception of a very few cases, sports takes away the violence that may occur between citizens across the city. For those who do not know, Chicago is a city that has a large collection of neighborhoods, and each neighborhood is like a city of its own. In past years, and even today in our city, you have to be careful and knowledgeable about specific elements as you enter certain areas and neighborhoods.

Proceeding through inner city neighborhoods is especially critical for black males, but basketball players, and other athletes are usually held in high esteem, and are even welcomed to visit any neighborhood to engage in competition. Basketball junkies, young and old just enjoy seeing talent. You can bet that wherever the best players are playing, they will attract a crowd. I would apply my previous statement to high school, college, or even Jr. high and grammar school. From year to year there is an ongoing debate that will last forever concerning who is the best high school player in the city. People even know who the best Jr. High and grammar school players are by 7th and 8th grade. Basketball is, and has always been an addiction for a large majority of city residents.

When I think of the hundreds and thousands of players who have come through this city's schools and playgrounds, I like to focus not on "what might have been", or the sad stories of blown opportunities, but on the many, many success stories that were encouraged along the way by being given an opportunity to succeed, or the chance to earn a college degree, and of course, all of those individuals who took advantage of the opportunities, including yours truly.

1936 is when the Chicago's Du Sable High School Panthers became the first all black high school to participate in the Illinois State High School Association Basketball State Championship tournament, but the 1953 team is the team that is referred to most frequently. That 1953 team featured Sweet" Charlie Brown the given star, who would later go to Seattle University and help lead them to the NCAA final four. Paxton Lumpkin was the magician who handled the ball so well that he wound up playing for the Harlem Globe Trotters later in his career. This Du Sable team played a brand of basketball at a pace that had never been seen at the state level. The fact that their fast break style had never been seen probably cost coach Jim Brown the state title during their second trip to the state tourney (1954). The officials had no idea of what was happening on the court. This team was so lightening quick, they figured a stutter (jab) step had to be traveling, or a steal had to be a foul. The panthers were defeated in the 1954 state championship game by a score of 76 –70. This DuSable Panthers team and coach Brown paved the way for many more Chicago teams that would come to the state tourney in the future. Du Sable was to be followed by many great teams and players over the years to carry on this proud, winning and competitive basketball tradition in the Chicago Public League. Let it never be forgotten that the school on 49th street started it all as far as showcasing black city players talents at the state tournament level. DuSable was located in what was always considered to be one of the toughest neighborhoods in the city, and was across the street from the notorious Robert Taylor Homes Housing Projects, which lined the state street corridor. Basketball has always been an extremely popular and attractive outlet for those who grew up in this area. Chicagoan Nat "Sweetwater" Clifton, the first black player to sign a contract with the National Basketball Association in 1950 is a DuSable alum. He played for the New York Knicks after playing with the Globe Trotters, and was a very imposing figure at 6'7" who could run the floor well. There were two other black players who played in the NBA in 1950. They were Chuck Cooper, who was the first black player drafted, and Earl Lloyd, who was the first black player to play in an NBA game. They faced many obstacles, but their success inspired many others to continue to seek to play basketball at the highest level in the NBA.Some of the top players who came through years later were: Zachary Blassingame, Kevin Porter (Bullets), Sam Gowers, Mitch Mosley, Maurice Cheeks (Sixers), Larry "Moon Cookie" Lewis (Philadelphia) who led the nation in rebounding while playing with Norm Van Lier at St. Francis of Loretto in Pennsylvania, Jimmy Odom, Stephon Butler, Brisbane "Jake" Harden, Bill Dise, Ray Bullocks, and Frank" Pearl" McFalls are other impact players from Du Sable. Even with all of the great players that have come through Du Sable and gone on to the professional ranks, as well as the European leagues, this school never won a city title after 1954, but played for the city title at least 5 times since 1954. This book will go further back to an era that began in the early 1900s at Phillips High School, which was the only black high school in Chicago at the time. You will come to realize how those players paved the way for the players of today. Yes, this is where and how it all started for the basketball playing millionaires of today's NBA who came out of Chicago. You have to think that there would be no millionaire contracts if not for the pioneers of basketball who we will talk about during this account of Chicago hoops history.

CHAPTER 3

INNER CITY HISTORY

The roaring twenties was when Phillips High School in Chicago on the south side of the city at 39th street at Pershing Road became an all black school. This is when people actually began to take notice, and realize that there was something special going on in the form of city basketball talent. Prior to that time Sam Ransom, a black 4 sport star had awed many while leading Hyde Park High School to championships in football, baseball, track, and basketball in 1901 - 1902. Basketball was his ticket to Beloit college where he performed in an outstanding fashion during his time there as a basketball star. Phillips, along with the Wabash YMCA located at 37th Street and Wabash Avenue, and the South Town YMCA located at 65th and Stewart Avenue were the places where the best players were developed during this period in the 1920s. Those 3 places are also known as **"The Golden Triangle"** according to well respected coach and historian Dr. Larry Hawkins." In the 20s and 30s, basketball was not divided into Varsity, Sophomore, or Freshman levels as it is today in our high schools. It was divided into two divisions: Heavy Weight (over 5'9") and Light weight (5'9" and under). Incidentally, our current Mayor Richard M. Daley, played in the lightweight division during the 1950s at De Lasalle Catholic High School in Chicago. The dramatic rise of the light weight division happened at Phillips in 1926 as the wildcats team made the semifinals of the public league championship before their spree was halted by Englewood which was an all white school during this time. (I know that's hard to believe for young readers, because Englewood has been all black for the last 40 years) This called attention to the black talented athletes who had started to play basketball in Chicago. Inman Jackson, a future Harlem Globe Trotter was the starting center on this team. Two years later, the Phillips lightweights returned and won the Public League Title by beating Harrison, which was considered to be a good team 23 – 10. Remember, this was when they still had a center jump ball after each made basket.

Basketball Historians, did you know that? Well historians, when James Naismith invented basketball, one of the rules was that each time a basket was scored, the clock was stopped and a center jump ball was to be held. (If you had a tall center, you'd have an advantage.) This tournament result opened even more eyes, because the media talked about how accurate the shooting was, and how fast the players played the game. The speed dazzled observers. Phillips had many rangy – fast players on the light weight squad. The player thought to be the best by many was Al "Runt" Pullins, another future Globe Trotter. The slow paced coaching philosophy probably shackled the players. They could have scored many more points if they were allowed to play the pace they liked, but the coach remained content to hold the ball, and protect their lead. They committed more fouls than Harrison because of their speed. The officials could not react fast enough to recognize what was happening as the defense forced the game to be played at a faster pace. Fast break, or up tempo basketball was on the way.

The Phillips Heavy Weight Team also was establishing the fact that they were hungry and dedicated to the desire of winning a city title. In 1924 they lost the heavy weight title game to Lane Technical High School, as Lane featured a black player as the high scorer. William Watson led the Lane Tech Indians over the Phillips Wildcats. Phillip's Heavy Weights would return two more times to the public league city semi final game, losing to Englewood both times.

Agis Bray, the 5'9" 140 team leader, and recognized by many to be the best athlete in the city during his time, led Phillips to a one point victory (20-19) over Morgan Park at the White City Arena as they finally won the city title in 1930. Bray was fast, extremely fast to the point where no other guard could match his speed. He also had a reputation for being a very good shooter. If someone described him during this time they would say: "He is fast and he is a pure shooter." Phillips had been the favorite since the beginning of the season. In 1930 the biggest post season tourney was not the state tourney, which was considered a tourney for downstate schools in the 30's. A few Chicago schools participated in the state tourney, but Phillips did not. The big post season tournament was the one held at the University of Chicago, and was called the Stagg National Tourney. The Public League Champion was given an automatic entry into this particular tournament every year, except in 1930 when Morgan Park, a white school received the automatic entry that Phillips should have received as the city champion. This was the only time that the racial injustice through segregation showed up in this fashion. Everyone accepted the fact that Phillips was not invited because their team was black. The Chicago Defender (a black publication) was the only newspaper that pointed out this blatant omission. The Stagg tourney included many teams that were from the Northern areas, who were still harboring a segregation mentality. They were threatening not to send their champions, if a black team was allowed to participate. Keeping Phillips from participating was really a way of keeping this tourney alive at the time, because teams would not have participated if Phillips had been invited. *Having to deal with these kinds of situations was common during this time period. Exclusions like this took place long before the Civil Rights Act of 1964 was passed, but it was another injustice that would have an effect on how things would change for the better in the future. This example just highlights the fact that even black basketball players have paid a price over the years for players to have the opportunities they have today. Even I feel that I have paid a price as the athletes before me did. The great thing is that every generation has helped to make it better for the next generation. That is why I appreciate history. I feel that everyone should be in touch with history, because the people whose experiences have impacted change helped to make America a better country. People like myself have benefitted greatly from the sufferage of those who lived before me who created, fought for, and made the best of the opportunities they had.*

A wise person once said: "How can you know where you're going if you don't know where you've been."

The given star, Agis Bray returned with the Phillips Wildcats again in 1931 as they defeated Bowen in the semifinals and went to the city title game seeking a victory which would give them two city titles in a row. They ran into the 6'8" Robert Gruenig of Crane Tech in the championship game. He won every center jump, and scored 17 points, as Crane defeated Phillips 30 – 2. Gruenig would later be elected to the Naismith National Basketball Hall of Fame. He was one of the great AAU stars of the 1930s. Bray went on to star at Wilberforce University in Ohio, and star on several semi professional teams in the 30s. Phillips participated in the National Black Schools Basketball Tourney in Hampton Virginia after their defeat in the city title game in 1931. The won the championship at Hampton Virginia by Defeating Virginia's Genoa West by a score of 30 – 14. The lightweight city champs of 1932 that featured my ex coach Charlie Gant, William McQuitter, Cleveland Bray, Leroy Rhodes, and Tilford Cole, who all went to Xavier University in New Orleans and compiled a record of 67 wins and 2 losses over a period of three years. All five starters were from Phillips. Bill McQuitter served as the assistant coach to Larry Hawkins's Carver teams in the early sixties that went to the state tourney two consecutive years. They won it during the second trip to state. Charlie Gant was the coach at Dunbar, Englewood, St. Elizabeth, and Douglas Elementary. What I will always remember about Charlie Gant is his motivational techniques. He would talk to you during running drills. He loved to start sentences with the word, sometimes. My favorite ones were: "Sometimes, you got to dig down deep. Sometimes, in the fourth quarter, you got to be in condition". "Sometimes, you got to make free throws and big shots when you're tired." Boy, did he make us mad with that. Imagine listening to that while running three miles. We really appreciated it during the season, as we were in better condition than most teams. You will never find a better, more dedicated teacher of basketball fundamentals than Charlie Gant. He passed on much knowledge of the game to people like myself, who I hope pass it along to the next group of players and coaches. I have always tried to pass on the fundamental teachings of Charlie Gant. A number of his methods were ingrained in me and affected many of the things I did while coaching, as they became a part of my philosophy. I guess I was fortunate to have good coaches and physical educators who all had an impact on my future instructional techniques. The list includes Chuck Frazier, Michael Clark, Jim Foreman, Fred Holman, and Leon Richardson. I once coached against Michael Clark at the high school level, (Du Sable vs. Manley) and beat him with his own out of bounds play, which I had learned from him 20 years earlier.

CHAPTER 4

PIONEERS OF THE GAME

According to historian Robert Pruters' "Early Phillips Teams" article, the talent produced by the Phillips teams in the twenties led to the development of one of the great organizations in basketball, who are presently known as the Harlem GlobeTrotters. As you've probably noticed, I've named a few individuals already who became members of the Globe Trotters. The first semi professional black team know in this area was the Savoy Big Five. The team consisted of many of the light weight and heavy weight stars from Chicago who played in the Public league during the 20s and 30s. Pruter discussed how Phillips had become the first black school in Chicago during the 20s.

Some of the stars were: Tommy Brookins, Lester Johnson, Randolph Ramsey, Walter "Toots" Wright, Inman Jackson, William Watson, Byron "Fat" Long, and William "Kid" Oliver. These are the pioneers that started it all at another level. In December of 1926, Abe Saperstein formed the Harlem Globe Trotters, who are still performing today as the international ambassadors of basketball. In 2004 I was part of a Globe Trotters horse competition with the media, and a ceremony where the Globe Trotters gave Phillips high school a large donation as they visited Chicago during their annual tour. It was totally appropriate because most of the original players came from Phillips high school.

The first team included a group from the Savoy Five that would later be joined by Al "Runt Pullins, Hillary Brown from Crane, and Nat "Sweetwater" Clifton from Du Sable High School. Remember, this is when no blacks were allowed to play in the NBA, and this was a chance to continue playing beyond college, and earn a little money. These players had jobs in addition to playing.

Chicago Happenings in the thirties:

While basketball was continuing to evolve during the 1930s, there are a number of other very significant historical events that occurred in 1933.

Chicago Mayor Anton Cermak was shot along with four others while making a public appearance with current president Franklin D. Roosevelt in Miami. He later died of his wounds, and the shooter was executed via electric chair. It is said that the shooting was retaliation for the shooting of Frank Nitty, Al Capone's hit man, which had taken place a year earlier. Other theorists say that the target was President Roosevelt.

22nd street in Chicago presently bears the name of Mayor

Cermak.

The first Major League Baseball AllStar game was played in Chicago at Comiskey Park, home of the Chicago White Sox in front of approximately 50,000 fans. The American League defeated the National league 4-2 on Babe Ruth's home run. Ring Lardner, known as the first baseball sports writer died in 1933 as well. He was known for writing about the 1919 Black Sox World Series scandal.

The first National Football League Championship game was played at Wrigley Field as the Chicago Bears defeated the New York Giants 23-21. They say it was very foggy that day as Papa Bear George Halas led the Bears to victory.

Chicago hosted the World's Fair as Speakeasies (now known as bars) continued to celebrate the end of prohibition. The Worlds Fair of 1933 sprawled from 12th street to 39th street along Chicago's lakefront. Some of the exciting activities included carnivals, sky-rides, rocket cars, alligator wrestling, dancers, and many other fun-filled events. Also, James Wedell flew a plane at a speed of around 300 miles per hour and set the world speed record in 1933.

There is no doubt that 1933 was a very interesting and exciting time in the history of the city of Chicago. Now, let me return to the main topic, "Inner City Hoops".

In 1936 DuSable, also known as the new Phillips broke through the segregation barrier and sent the first all black team to play in the state high school tournament which was held in Champaign Illinois. Things had changed for the better in our great state.

CHAPTER 5

THE 1950'S

The fifties has to be the hey day of basketball for the inner city, and the public league. This is when many things started to change. Players were still developing and getting opportunities to go to college via athletic scholarship. Many players went to black universities, but many were attending white universities in larger numbers than ever. Also, the NBA was getting ready to include black players in the league. Tilden High, the alma mater of Johnny "Red" Kerr, he of Chicago Bulls and Minneapolis Laker fame won the city in 1950, Parker High took it in 1951, and Roosevelt High won the city in 1952. They were all defeated in the state tourney in the first round. DuSable won in consecutive seasons (1953 and 1954), and advanced to the state championship game in 1954 to lose 76 – 70 to Mount Vernon. It was a major achievement. No city team had gone as far. There was more to come. Marshall won city and lost in the first round of the state tourney in 1955. The city was represented by Dunbar in the year 1956. Al "Peg" Saunders was the shooter who led the scoring in Dunbar's only city championship basketball season. They would go on to finish 3rd in the state tournament. Mel Davis a future Harlem Globe Trotter was the big man who exerted his dominance with his 6'7" 260 pound frame. He is a guy who gave a great deal back to the community with the summer camps he always hosted during the summers at Dunbar high school. I was one of the kids who benefited from those camps at Dunbar along with many other kids. He also gave us free Pro Keds basketball shoes. When we paid for them as members of our high school team they were only $4 per pair during the season. This was due to Mel's influence. Thanks Mel.

The guards at Dunbar who played on the title team were Bob "Quick" Watkins and Hank Clark. Bernard Mills the scorer of the future at that time was still being groomed for greatness. There were a number of outstanding players in this era. Rufus Calhoun, Abe Booker, Ron Beavers, Mac Irvin, and George Pruitt were some of the highest scoring players around who put up huge numbers in not only the high school games, but the leagues and open gym sites all around the city.

George Wilson led the Marshall Commandos to the first state championship won by a Chicago team in 1958. A very dominant player, Wilson was unstoppable as Isadore "Spin' Salario allowed this team to play the playground brand of basketball which is technically know as up tempo. M.C. Thompson was a strong member of Wilson's supporting cast who contributed along with Steve Thomas and Charlie Jones. Marshall would return several more times to state, as a matter of fact, they won the city championship 4 times in a row from 1958-1961. First it was George Wilson, then it was Shaky Jake and others who led the Commandos. In the future they would return under hall of fame coach Luther Bedford several times to become the team that appeared the most times at the state tourney. The most memorable times would be under coach Bedford with a 6'2" center (Joe Stiffend) and again with the Hoop Dreams camera crew following every game of the city championship season during the documentary that became a national story.

Crane was the city champ in 1957 and was beaten by Evanston Township in the first round.

CHAPTER 6

THE 1960'S

Darius "Pierre" Cunningham of Carver scored over 50 points at least five times, including games of 90, and 67 points. Future number 1 draft choice of the New York Knicks, the great Cazzie Russell who led Carver high coached by Larry "Legend" Hawkins to the state title game in 1962 was a 6'6"scoring machine. They lost that game to Decatur, but returned the next season without Cazzie to win it all after defeating Centralia for the state championship in 1963 by one point as Joe Allen led the scoring, but reserve Anthony Smedley heaved a buzzer shot through the hoop from the opposite free throw line to win the game. (63-62) It was poetic justice for Coach Hawkins who lost the previous season's state title game by a single point in the waning seconds. Cazzie Russell went on to Michigan and set all kinds of records which was followed by a successful NBA career. He was the first Chicago-bred number 1 draft pick in the NBA.

Crane and Dan Davis won the city in 1964, but Marshall surfaced again to win the city in 1965 and1966. Harlan won it 3 times (1967, 1970-71) Crane took it in 1968.

The first black NBA player was Nat "Sweetwater" Clifton who played at Du Sable high in Chicago, (of course) and also with the Harlem Globe Trotters.

The 1960s had many scorers. 5'10" point guard Bill Saxton of Parker high led the Public League in scoring in 1961 with an average of 25.5 points per game in his junior year. Remember this was before the 3 point line . Longtime coach Wilford Bonner told Saxton to shoot every chance he had, because he was such a deadly shooter. He duplicated his 25ppg average in his senior year and went on to Wilberforce University in Ohio on a full ride.

Sonny Parker has to be mentioned from the seventies. After starring at Farragut high in Chicago, he went on to have a stellar career with the Golden State Warriors.

Mickey Johnson of Lindblom high also quietly had a successful NBA career. Not many have given of their time and expertise as Sonny Parker has. I respect him for that.

1969 featured probably the best scorer/shooter ever in the history of high school basketball. Billy "the kid" Harris was a gunslinger who averaged 40 points per game. The remarkable thing is that not only was there no 3 point line, all of his shots came from deep out on the perimeter.

At 6'2" Billy could also take it to the hoop and dunk on you. He had an uncanny ability to get his shot off from anywhere on the court. He would shoot from as far as 40 feet out. A number of times he stepped over half court and let it fly. His one handed release is legendary. His most amazing game was his 57 point effort at DuSable in 1969 to break the Panthers winning streak in their gym (Panther Paradise). The kid never made it as big as he could have. He was the MJ of his day. He was drafted by the Chicago Bulls, and was the last player cut that year. He later played for the old ABA San Diego Conquistadors.

CHAPTER 7

THE 1970'S

The seventies was when Chicago really intensified its basketball love. Many things came about during this time. Some of the products were: Isaiah Thomas, Mark Aguirre, Eddie Johnson, Glenn "Doc" Rivers, Ronnie Lester, Bo Ellis, Rickey Green, Carl Nicks, Ken Dancy, Sherrod Arnold, Marty "Jo-Jo" Murray, Robert Byrd, Darius Clemmons, Larry "Jab" Williams and many more.

The Chicago Neighborhood Basketball League also known as CNBL. It was held outside only during the summer. It was also citywide and allowed every neighborhood park or playground to field a team. Around 100 teams with players between the ages of 15 and 18 would play every summer. The championship was played on the outdoor court at Lake Meadows Park and was televised. The winning team's best five would represent Chicago in the Boston Shoot Out which was held for players who were 17 years old and under at that time. The remainder of the team was selected by tryouts held by Chicago Park District Physical Education Supervisors James Albritton, and famous official (first black to officiate the state championship series) Reuben Norris who is one of the alltime best officials along with Nate Humphries and Malcolm Hemphill. Mau Mau Cason came along later, but is also among the best.

These guys are the best officials because they are true teachers of the game, as well as keepers of the game. They are all members of the Chicago – founded African American M.O.A., which is the Midwest Officials Association.

Mayor Daley's Neighborhood Program came on after CNBL and was basically the same type of league. It was played on every outdoor court in every neighborhood across the city, only during the summer. A champion would always be determined in August, and you could look for that team to be very competitive during the high school season. It was a rule. If you did well in the summer, everyone would expect you to be in the thick of things during the high school season. The competition was everything you could ask for as a spectator. The creativity is still seen today. Many of the moves that are unbelievable today were done back then. Even players with the hang time and the grace of Michael Jordan were seen back then. Shooting is an art that was mastered by a number of players in this era. A sweet touch was seen frequently back in the day. There have been many players who could jump as high as anyone or shoot as well as anyone, but did not make the NBA for other reasons.

We will mention them as we continue.

The Chicago Park District League also began to go full force at this time during the winter. Every park was represented on 2 levels (12-14 and 15-18). This was a great developmental league for future high school players as well as players who were in high school and were not playing varsity for one reason or another. The city championship was a very big accomplishment. I have the dubious honor of participating on multiple city park district championship teams on both levels.

In 1970 Charles Frazier, Phys Ed. teacher at Douglas Elementary started a school team called the Douglas Allstars. He also started an all school intramural league that was played during lunch hour every day. Every seventh and eighth grade classroom had a team participating. I bet he did not know that the kids he selected for the all stars, schooled, and played year round with would become state champions in six years. Well they did in 1975 at Phillips High School under Herb Brown with Frazier as an assistant as you will read about later.

In the 1971 Xmas tourney at the old UIC gymnasium on 12th street and Roosevelt Road on the near west side, Donnie Von Moore, Donnel Hunt, and Kenwood defeated Parker to win the championship as Bo Ellis's last second turn around fade away shot rimmed out.

I'll always remember the sportsmanship Bo displayed

while shaking hands with Kenwood after the tough loss. That's the kind of character I want to develop in our student athletes of today. In 1973 Hirsch high returned to the city with the state title. They were led by Ricky Green, a future Michigan all American who became a number 1 draft choice of the golden state warriors.

John Robinson who also attended Michigan was probably the best 6'5" center ever, was a force for this Hirsch team and coach Charlie Stimpson. Joshua Smith and Robert Brooks also contributed big time to this state championship. They were the first champions who I saw speak on TV. I remember them saying "Hi Mom" during their interviews On TV after winning it all. I got a big kick out of that. Their comments caught on, and many celebrated athletes gave the same salute to their Moms during interviews I saw in the future. These players were products of the south side playgrounds, specifically Chatham YMCA, Avalon Park, Grand Crossing Park, and Avalon Playground. The thing about playground play back in the day was that you could not play as loose on the school team as you did on the playground. You had to adapt your game, because certain things, especially hot dogging was not allowed. I know many great playground players who never made the school team because they couldn't adjust their games, or couldn't make their grades. I believe that the discipline of my time was much much tougher. For example, it was acceptable to paddle players for mistakes, as well as for behavior and other disciplinary reasons. I'll never forget the fiber glass paddle that Ray Price used regularly for missed lay-ups. I made sure I made all of my lay-ups and free throws whenever he pulled it out. He made us tough, and was a strong advocate of "killer instinct."

Hirsch defeated the tough Parker Colonels at the Amphitheater in Chicago to win the city. Parker featured Maurice "Bo" Ellis, the 6'9" 26ppg scorer who scored 30 in defeat, and went on to Marquette University for 2 final 4 appearances and 1 national championship and then to the Denver Nuggets. Bo Ellis learned to play at Hamilton Park near 71st Street under Mr. Richardson, the Park Director. AlFredrick Hughes who also played at Parker (which became Robeson) and starred at Loyola before being drafted by the San Antonio Spurs in the first round, also honed his skills at the same south side park and playground locations.

In 1972 Dan Davis, former Crane High and Northwestern University star coached Crane to the city title with great players who learned to play at west side locations such as Dr. King's Boys Club, Marrillac House, New berry Center, and New City YMCA. The star of this team was Nate Williams. The supporting cast was loaded, but young. They were ball wizard and scorer Andre "Champ" Wakefield and shooter James Jackson, two big time players who attended Loyola and

Minnesota respectively. Wakefield dabbled with several NBA teams (Detroit, Chicago, and Indiana) He thrilled crowds with his shake and bake moves and his hang time. He loved to say his name as an announcer would after a made jump shot as he let it go from the corner. "Waaakefielddd"

1974 was the year that Levi Cobb, then a sophomore led the Morgan Park Mustangs to the city championship by defeating Phillips in the old International Amphitheater. DuSable who had future 76er Maurice Cheeks, Dilbert Blasingame, Frank "Pearl" McFalls, Ray Bullocks, and Bill Dise, lost in the semi finals.

The Du Sable players developed in the Chicago Park District's Robert Taylor Park, and The Community Center/Boys Club. There was also an area on south state street known as the Hole that was known for producing the city's best point guards. Mo Cheeks, Kevin Porter, and Stephon Butler are 3 pretty good ones from there.

Morgan Park lost at the state tourney in 1974, but would return in two years as seniors to win it all in 1976 and give Chicago back to back state champions. Luck was really on their side as they defeated Dunbar in the city quarter finals at Corliss high school in 1976 by one point, which I never will forget. Our team manager found a rabbits foot under their bench after the game. I remember the emotion I felt as approximately 1,000 fans waited for us and applauded as we filed off the bus that night after returning to Dunbar High School after an extremely tough loss that night. There were many tears shed.

They also won the state championship game by one point on a buzzer shot.

Basketball was really hot well before the bulls were winning any championships. Long before Michael Jordan, Chicagoans loved to play and watch hoops. That is one reason why they could really appreciate a player like MJ who I have to acknowledge as the best, period.

CHAPTER 8

HOT SPOTS IN THE CITY

D r. King Boys Club and Chicago State University were two spots where the summer league action was outstanding. All college, pro, and European players from Chicago would come home annually and put on a free show in the summer time during the seventies. Some of the European and NBA pros were: Marcellous Starks, Mitchell JJ Anderson, Steve King, Sidney Cobb, Charles Brakes, Arthur Sivels, Voise Winters, Bobby Wilson, Billy Harris, Donald Reese, Sonny Parker, Johnny Bee Williams, Lee Arthur Scott, Sherwen "The Enforcer" Moore and others. College stars were: Terry Cummings, Ken Dancy, Isaiah Thomas and Ronnie Lester who both played on the 1979 Pan American gold medal winning team for Bobby Knight, Glenn Rivers, and Mark Aguirre who scored a record number of points on several hot steamy nights in the summer league at Chicago State. Eddie Johnson, Darryl "Sky" Walker, the skinny high jumping kid from Corliss High who went to the NBA and later became a coach, Stephon Butler, Kenny "The Snake" Norman, Nezzie Hurst, Mickey Johnson, and more.

Where were all these players learning to play so well? Not summer camps. They were learning in the neighborhoods. The most creative passes, shots, and other moves were developed on the playground or at other inner city locations.

Navy Pier, located on the lake just northeast of downtown Chicago was a place you could go and play all day against players from all over the city. They'd give you a tag after you put your clothes in a wire basket and we'd play until dark, get back on the Wacker Avenue bus and go home. This was an experience to treasure. The neighborhood guys would have the goal of going to Navy Pier, and staying on the court all day without losing. The Pier had about 20 full courts, enough to accommodate players from all over. They had a picture of Bunny Leavitt on the wall. He was the guy who made over 1,000 free throws in a row.

Douglas playground on 32nd Street was a hotbed of sorts in the seventies. Known for their daily competitive play, and outdoor tournaments run by Playground teachers of the old Shelter House. Zeke Green, Mr. Cozy, Watson Robertson, and the late Ms. Cooley. Players from all around would come to play there to see if they could dominate the court. It was normal to leave if you lost a game because there were so many people waiting to play, you would not play again if you lost. So again, the object was to stay on the court by winning as many games as possible.

Anderson Playground, Madden Park Homes (Ida B Wells), Williams Park (Dearborn Homes), Henry Booth House (Ickes), Stateway Gardens Park, and Hilliard Playground (Hilliard Homes) all had the same flavor, the same competitiveness.

One of my favorite outdoor tourneys in the summer time was held in the Hilliard Homes housing development. It was financed by a group called IPACAC. The action was outstanding every summer. For about two weeks the best of the city's finest high school aged players would go at it from sun up to sun down. Players would hear about each other and travel to opponents playgrounds to compete against them. Marcus Liberty, Ronnie Lester, Carl Golston, Herman Hoskins, Greg Parham, Steve Parham, Mango Cline, Charles Brakes, Jeffrey Allen, Arthur Sivels, Len Tolliver, Larry Harper, Clyde (Lew Alcindor) Davis, Sylvester "Oily" Thomas, Sherrod Arnold, Dwight "Butter" Williams, Larry Murray, Marty "JoJo" Murray,(a 4 sport all city player) Tyrone Bradley, Darius Clemmons,

And Ricky Wilks (the kid whose family moved from 33rd street to Batavia after 8th grade) are a few who played at these south side locations. Two of the best west side players were Mike Johnson (brother of Eddie) and Lamar Mondane and his legendary long distance jump shot.

Many of the players from these neighborhoods earned scholarships and professional contracts, but the publicity they received was nothing close to what the media exposure is today.

Back in the day self esteem could be built on the court. There's no better feeling than to know you're one of the best in the neighborhood among your peers. Everyone would shoot and the first two persons to make a free throw would choose sides. If you got to the point where you didn't have to shoot to play on a team, you knew you were good. If you were selected on the way into the playground, you knew you were very good, and if someone came to your house to get you, you knew you were one of the best. It could be brutal waiting to play next game. The object of playing was to keep winning and stay on the court as long as possible. The winners got to continue to play. The losers had to leave the court after every game. My friend and neighbor Fat Willoughby and I had a goal of staying on the court all day every day, and we did most of the time. The older guys played us very physical and bent the rules to their advantage, but it made us tough. We were the two tallest kids in the neighborhood in our teenage years. I was 6'3", and he was 6'1". Interestingly enough, he was really skinny, but I found out they called him "Fat" because he was fat when he was a baby. We owned the Douglas playground court on most days. There was plenty of trash talking daily. The most stinging trash talk was yelled out after game ending shots. My favorites were:

"In your eye", face job, "Next", "Game time", "Money, and "Yo face." It was all in fun most of the time. Bragging rights were worth a million dollars in the neighborhood. If you

could beat someone on the court, the respect you would get
was unbelievable.

There's no play like playground play. There are no calls
like playground calls. They don't call carrying the ball like
they used to. Never back (young players might not have heard
of this) was a regular call in the half court when a missed shot
was not taken past the free throw line prior to shooting for the
basket. "First" was called to settle all held balls/jump balls.
Whoever called first, first got possession of the ball.

CHAPTER 9

THE TOP CITY LEAGUE

O f all of the leagues throughout the city, the Summer-Pro-League was, and still is today, the best, most prestigious, competitive league in the city of Chicago. I would go even further and compare it to any of the top leagues across the country. I think its better than the Rucker League in New York, and The Sonny Viccaro League in the Philadelphia Area. In the opinion of many, it is better than the NBA Rookie league that is held in the summer. It is the best because the best players have played here since the league began in the 70s. This includes professional players who live in the area as well as professionals who visit Chicago. Some of the top college players are involved in this league, along with a number of European players and CBA (Continental Basketball League) players. Chicago has so many pros, that when they return home during the summer this league gives them an opportunity to stay in shape, and to entertain the home folks, family, and friends. It is really something to see. These games are much more entertaining than many NBA games. The league would be a great place to create an all time highlight reel. Pros like Mark Aguirre, Isaiah Thomas, Glenn Rivers, Billy Harris, Ronnie Lester, Ricky Green, Jeff Wilkins, Maurice "Bo" Ellis, Quinn Buckner, Lloyd and Boyd Batts, Lee Arthur Scott, Artis Gilmore, Reggie Theus, Darryl "Sky" Walker, Terry Cummings, Sonny Parker, Mickey Johnson, JJ Anderson, Tim Hardaway, Tony Brown, Randy Brown, Eddie Johnson, and Kenny "Snake" Norman helped to attract record crowds to gyms around the city. The player who's introduction was always the best was Eddie Hughes when the announcer, "In The Gym" Jimmie Smith would say "The Jumpingest, The Quickest, The 5'10" dynamo from Austin High and Colorado State,

Eddieeeeeee Huuughess". This was pure basketball entertainment at its best. Michael Jordan even played during several summers. He scored about 60 one night. It was so crowded in the IIT gym that you couldn't see the baselines, or the sidelines. Of course Michael still proceeded to go baseline and score whenever he felt like it. Other all stars like Earvin "Magic" Johnson, Patrick Ewing, and Charles Barkley have also played in the Chicago Summer Pro League. This league started in the 70s at Dr. Martin Luther King Jr boys club, and Malcolm X College, both are located on the near west side of Chicago. The league was later moved to a larger facility to accommodate the large over flowing crowds. That facility was the old Chicago State University gymnasium located at 95th

Street and King Drive on the far South Side of the City. It has since moved to De Lasalle High School, and is currently held at The Illinois Institute of Technology at 31st and State Street, that great street on the near south side.

The league runs from June through mid August every summer. Games are played on three evenings a week. On the average, there are 3-4 games per day. The most surprising thing about this league is that admission is free. That's amazing, because the action is so entertaining that if someone wanted to charge fans for admission, the league would be very profitable. This is a league where you can make a name for yourself. If a player plays well here, he has a good chance of playing in the NBA. Many players have earned ten day contracts, and European contracts from their performances in this league. The most heartwarming thing about the summer pro league is that it brings people together. Basketball just seems to eliminate all conflicts and differences. Rich, Poor, or Middle Class, you find all kinds of people in attendance. They all have the same desire at these games: To enjoy the action and have a great time. You will see more standing ovations at this league than any other. The memories are great as well. I remember the night that Isaiah Thomas got a standing ovation for missing all three of his free throws back when you were given three to make two for a foul in the back court under the old NBA rules that they used. He was awarded a bogus foul that would have decided the game as the game was tied with no time remaining. He decided to miss all three purposely, and send the game to overtime. He received a standing ovation for prolonging a great game that night which his team eventually lost. I also remember the night that Mark Aguirre was given technical foul for kicking the ball into the bleachers. He really focused after that and went on to score a tournament record 63 points that night against the B&H Allstars and Artis Gilmore. He left the game to a standing ovation. I have a vivid memory of the night that Billy Harris took over a close game at Dr. King Boys Club with 3, 30 foot jump shots and a slam dunk in a crowded lane down the stretch to earn a standing ovation and win the game for the Presidents Lounge sponsored team. He called himself "Downtown Brown" that night while sipping on an orange soda after the game. Freddie "Downtown" Brown was one of the hottest shooters in the NBA at that time while playing for Seattle.

CHAPTER 10

MORE 1970'S

In 1975 the state champion was Phillips high school. They defeated Morgan Park in a payback game from the previous year. Coached by Herb Brown, they played all out pressure with double teams all over the floor. Even a good point guard would wilt under the pressure before the game was over. This team was capable of a quick spurt that would end the game early. They could also play four corners or the shuffle cut-delay game with the best of them. If you got behind, you'd be in trouble. The plan was play tough defense, get the ball to Larry "Jab" Williams in the post for the left handed turnaround, or kick it out to Vincent "Dimp" Robinson for the perimeter jump shot. This was the year that Chuck Frazier's original Douglas all stars were seniors. His year round work had paid off. 10 tournaments a year is what he did with his players. He was ahead of his time because he was playing an AAU schedule in the off season before AAU was in existence with his year round dedication and commitment to player development. Ex Douglas all stars on this team were Larry "Jab" Williams, Marty "Jo-Jo" Murray, Robert Byrd,

Darius "Poodle" Clemmons, Louis Reymond, and Lavon "Nut" Richmond. Other key members of that state championship team were Ike deal, Dorian "Bill" Figgers, Teddy James, and Herman Hoskins. Can you tell that yours truly was a Douglas all star too. So was Ronnie Lester, Ricky Wilks, Al Redmond, and many others. The Phillips wildcats returned to the state championship tourney after winning the city in 1977 when Herb Brown was promoted to Basketball Coordinator for the Chicago Public Schools, and Chuck Frazier became head coach at Phillips. Again there was a number of Douglas all stars on the squad: Sherrod Arnold, Tyrone Bradley, Carl Golston, William "Truly" Smith, and Bernard Jackson. All of these kids received scholarships as their dedication and hard work paid off.

There were many other places where talent was developed in the seventies:

Old Town Boys Club on the west side at 12th and Taylor Street, Fosco Park in "the village", and Dr. Martin Luther King Boys Club, on the near west side (Sacramento Avenue) were places where the north west south and east sides of the city would play in the citywide 12 and under biddy winter tourney. As a member of the Magicians, we defeated a team from Logan Square 102 to 2. We never took the press off. David "Road Runner" Taylor, James "Moo Moo" Moore, Pierce "Boochie" Cole, Ron Lester and Myself were all involved with this game that featured a 2-2-1 press that never allowed them to score a field goal (they scored two free throws) . The coach Mike Clark was never criticized for leaving the press on the entire game. Times have changed. He would be criticized today, because there were many tears shed by the team that was totally embarrassed. We just thought of it as a team having fun. We had no mercy, and took pride in having a high level of killer instinct. Anyone who has ever played knows that it's a whole lot of fun especially for the substitutes of the team that's winning to score in a lopsided game. When you're young kids you don't realize that burying a team is probably not a good sportsmanlike thing to do. I certainly would not condone it or enjoy it today. Sportsmanship really is important. All young players should practice good sportsmanship whether you win or lose.

Other locations across the city hosted these games. They were Woodlawn Boys Club on 63rd Street East, Chatham YMCA on 83rd Street (who were coached by John "Buck" Paul) and at the Wabash YMCA on 37th street which was run by Bob Hansen and Clarence Nelson. We won the tourney and were allowed to travel to Kansas City and Indiana to compete with other teams in the Midwest. We always did well. We played basketball everyday. If there was no game, we practiced or played recreationally. Mike Clark, the first of the AAU coaches assemble the best talent from a number of different schools to form a team first called the magicians, and later becoming the Jr. Globe Trotters during this time. The trotters were known all over the city as a collection of the best players. We could beat anybody, anywhere, anytime, and anyplace, but the hundreds of teams around the city never stopped trying. Beating the trotters was a big deal, so whenever it happened you would hear about it all around the neighborhoods. We won many championship trophies from pretty much any and every tournament in Chicago, and even outside of Chicago. This explains why so many ex trotters played basketball at the college and professional levels. All of us were from humble beginnings and basketball gave us college scholarship opportunities. Many of our lives have been changed in a positive fashion because we took advantage of the opportunities that basketball made possible. The trotters were the first club team to acquire uniforms with players names on the back, and suede red converse all star shoes. A few members of the trotters were selected to play in the National Biddy Tournament in Puerto Rico when we were 12 years old. Biddy basketball was played all over the city in the 70s just as it is today. A Jr. Trotters basketball team reunion was held in July of 2006. It was amazing to see how many of the men were successful, and were giving back to kids. Many of them were coaches, counselors, teachers, school administrators, journalists, police commanders, detectives, NBA scouts and assistant general managers. At the reunion luncheon and game which was played at Dunbar high school, there were 7 all Americans, final four and NCAA national championship game winners, NBA championship winners, and 5 NBA draft choices who came back to honor coach Clark, and contribute donations to his current high school, which is Collins High School located on the west side of Chicago. Approximately 10,000 was donated at the luncheon, and the game was outstanding. The message throughout the weekend was that coach Clark was not only an AAU pioneer before its time, he had actually impacted the lives of many many young men in a very positive way, and many of them were giving back to inner city kids the same way Michael had given to them. It turned into a weekend of gratitude to Michael Clark who had done so much for so many. What a pleasure it was to see all of the guys come together after about 30 years. It was truly one of the most positive experiences I've had in basketball.

30 Years Later

Above is a post game group photo from the reunion game in July 2006 after the blue squad blew out the red squad. Yours truly (standing in the middle for the winning Blue Team) pumped in 20. Third highest total to JJ Anderson's 28, and Ken Dancy's 25. Ronnie Lester chipped in with 22 assists.

Included here is an article about the weekend Fundraiser Reunion Luncheon and Game that was written by Tony Brooks and published by Black Sports The magazine: I thought it is very appropriate to include Tony's article. He played an interesting role of observer and participant throughout the weekend.

FROM BOYS TO MEN - THANK YOU MICHAEL CLARK

By Tony Brooks

They came from around the country to honor and re-unite with their friend and former coach. These former Jr. Trotters traveled to Chicago from coast to coast, as far east as Washington, D.C., and as far west as California, from Madison, Wisconsin to as far south as Memphis, Tennessee. This two day event was conceptualized by former Jr. Trotters and Paul Lawrence Dunbar high school teammates Calvin Davis – Director of Sports Administration for the Chicago Public Schools and Ronnie Lester – Assistant General Manager of the NBA Los Angeles Lakers.

Who is Michael Clark? He is a 56 year old Chicago Southside basketball coaching legend, deserving of a statue being erected in his likeness at Anderson Park, although it has not been done yet. Clark was recently honored at a benefit luncheon and basketball game by several of his former players known as the Jr. Trotters. The Jr. Trotters were AAU level basketball players organized by Clark in the late 1960's, before the term AAU Basketball went vogue.

Clark's core players were mainly from the Bronzeville/Gap community, stretching from 29th street to 39th street – Cottage Grove to State Street. Michael Clark was a man from the

"Hood" who genuinely cared about the boys in the "Hood" and became the father-figure/friend that many of his players never had.

Clark was not a rich philanthropist with idle time and a hoops hobby, he was quite the opposite. He was a square-dancer with a jalopy of a car, who stumbled into coaching. As Clark began to assemble his future dream team of defensive specialist and offensive dagger-masters from the Chicago Housing Authority's - Dearborn Homes, Ida B. Wells, Stateway Gardens, and such like, he somehow-someway provided gym shoes, uniforms, transportation and friendship without taking one nickel from them or their parents.

Before Clark had his notorious lime-green AMC Hornet car, he set out on foot walking door-to-door from Cermak to 29th street looking for sponsors to provide the necessities to dress out his team. The *Chicago Defender* newspaper company was the first to open a door and invite Clark in. Burger King soon followed, and the Jr. Trotters were off and trotting, neighborhood-to-neighborhood, city-to-city, state-to-state. Eventually, the Harlem Globetrotters became a sponsor. The Jr. Trotters often played the warm up game before the Harlem Globetrotters took to the court when passing through Chicago.

Human beings can do some pretty amazing things, and Michael Clark is one of those amazing people. When Clark's former players began to file into the reception hall at the Martinique Restaurant and reminisce, the amazing Michael Clark stories revived.

Kenton "Tiger" Rainey who is now the Assistant Chief of Police in Whittier California recalled Clark's 1970's era green Hornet with no seat belts, an open hole in the floorboard and a seating capacity that could seemly cram in a bus load of teen-agers. Rainey noted, "If Clark did that today, he would be locked up." Tyrone "T-Bone" Bradley remembered Clark making his players drill against one another one-on-one the full length of the basketball court. He also remembered the left hand only dribble drills.

More importantly though, Clark taught him how to trust in and help people. Referring to Clark, Bradley said, "He was always in the community at Anderson playground playing basketball with us." Without Clark in their lives, Bradley said the boys in the hood would be 'bangin' and 'drugin'. "He never asked for anything" said Bradley.

Bradley showed up at the Jr. Trotters training camp going into his sophomore year at Chicago's Wendell Phillips high school. During his sophomore season playing varsity basketball at Phillips, Bradley's team was ranked # 1 in the Chicago Public League with a 29-0 record. Phillips played and beat the # 2 ranked Westinghouse team for the Public League Championship. Westinghouse featured future NBA # 1 draft pick Mark Aguirre, along with Eddie Johnson and Skip Dillard. Bradley finished out his Jr. Trotters career as a 1978-79 All-Star. His All-Star teammates included three future NBA Players: Mitchell "JJ" Anderson, Glenn "Doc" Rivers, Terry Cummings and McDonald's All-American Teddy Grubbs.

Standing five-feet - nine inches tall and weighing 105 pounds as a high school senior, Bradley received a four year basketball scholarship to Fresno State University. He played his last college game in his senior year at Madison Square Garden winning the NIT Championship. Being a realist with his 5'9" height, "T-Bone" bowed out of the NBA draft camps and completed his Bachelors degree in Criminology and went on to earn a Masters in Counseling, which became his chosen profession in the Fresno School District. For his dedication to running a youth basketball camp along with Golden State Warriors GM Rod Higgins and Bobby Anderson, Bradley has been awarded four keys to the city of Fresno over the years.

The luncheon ceremonies for Michael Clark tipped off at 2pm with Albert Sharp as Master of Ceremonies, and Isaac Carter welcomed everyone. Calvin Davis gave the statement of the occasion, and then several former Jr. Trotters gave their reflections of Clark.

Ronnie "Santo" Lester took his first organized basketball baby steps with Michael Clark's Jr. Trotters Biddy Basketball team. Lester, who later became a University of Iowa Hawkeye All-American and won two NBA Championships playing with Magic Johnson and Kareem Abdul-Jabbar, credited Clark with being where he is today. When Mitchell "JJ" Anderson (Asst. Coach – Memphis Grizzles) came to the podium, he introduced himself and stated, "As a high school senior at Metro, I averaged 45 points a game and led the nation in scoring. Playing for Clark, I averaged 5 points a game and learned to play defense."

Anderson gave Clark a lot of love during his brief remarks, as did all of the former players who commented before and after him. "JJ" concluded his remarks with a pledge of $1,000.00 to the Chicago Public Schools.

Closing in on the 4:00 hour, Sherrod Arnold was called upon to introduce Michael Clark. Arnold came to the podium with his love story. He too remembered Clark's green Hornet with the hole in the floorboard. When the team would throw their equipment in the car, sometimes their gear would fall out through the hole. Arnold recalled a road trip where Clark had to back up on Lake Shore Drive because someone's gym shoe fell out through the hole, and he had to retrieve it, because there were no extra gym shoes to spare. Arnold also reflected on when he joined up with the Jr. Trotters, his gym shoe had a hole in it and Clark got him a new pair. Before taking his seat, Sherrod Arnold told of his educational and career accomplishments, and then, he threw down a verbal commitment of $500.00 to benefit the Chicago Public Schools.

Michael Clark was given a special presentation plaque award by his former players, which he humbly and graciously accepted while giving some love back to his boys who have become men - caring and successful men.

The following day, Saturday at high noon, at Paul Lawrence Dunbar Vocational High School, two big boxes outside of the gymnasium entrance contained red and blue numbered T-Shirts labeled Jr. Trotters 2006 Basketball Reunion. A showdown of legends was-a-brewing, with Michael Clark standing at the door passing out the T-Shirts and "stacking" his Blue Team. His opposing coach was none other than former Jr. Trotter and Phillips alum Robert Byrd. Byrd helped his 1975 Wildcats team win a state championship, and then he traveled on to Marquette University and won a NCAA national championship in 1977 with legendary coach and character builder – Al McGuire.

Clark quickly targeted former Jr. Trotters who graduated from Dunbar. They were: 6-5 Ken Dancy, who played professionally in Europe for 18 years; 6-3 Calvin Davis who played in the back-court with 6-2 Ronnie Lester, teamed up again after 30 years; Former quarterback Brian Jordan who is the Asst. Chief of Police in D.C. suited up in the familiar blue as did another Asst. Chief of Police (Non Dunbar Alum)

Kenton Rainey. The remaining non-Dunbar alumni were Manley's Donnie Kirksey, along with Phillips and Princeton grad Dr. Kenneth Cline.

For the Red Team – Robert Byrd had good ingredients to mix in his stew. 6-7 Teddy James was a Phillips and Marquette teammate of Byrd's with a high school state championship and college national championship under his belt; Phillips All-Stater and NIT champion Tyrone Bradley wore red along with another Phillips legend 6-6 Steve Parham. When 6-8 "JJ" Anderson walked in, he too was handed a red T-Shirt, but Clark somehow orchestrated a trade and "JJ" started on the Blue Team; Phillips alumni Eugene Brown, Stu Gibson, Anthony Jackson, Ted Sanders and William Smith, along with Harper high's Demetrius Williamson, rounded out the Red Team line-up. Free-lance journalists witness some thrilling events when duty calls, so even yours truly donned a red # 2 T-Shirt and subbed for the often winded middle-aged time-outters.

The game was fun to watch, even though it was not at the warp speed it would have been played at 30 years ago. The Pros looked every bit of it. Washington Bullets draftee Ken Dancy, at 48 years old still has a prime time package of a game. He put up five left-handed three pointers and five more short ranged buckets for 25 points. Ronnie Lester's smile could not be wiped off his face, he was so happy to be back at his alma-mater with his childhood friends. As for his game, it was as smooth as expensive silk, and very easy on the eyes. He tallied 10 points and had a monster number of assist. *Calvin Davis, still looking spry at 48 years young contributed 20 points for the blue team on a variety of shots which redeemed him after he missed a breakaway lay-up after the opening tip.* "JJ" Anderson at 45 years old is still a dangerous adversary who gave a demonstration of how he became national scoring champ in 1978. Of his 28 points, he dropped three – three point long range bombs on the Red Team to help establish a dazzling-quick, never-look-back commanding lead. After the Dancy/Anderson aerial bombardment slowed down, Coach Byrd called a time out for the Red Team that looked mesmerized. Clark was basking in the glory days of old, while Byrd pointed out to his team that they basically had no offense, and no defense. In fact, Byrd said with a big smile and a laugh, it was the first time he had ever seen a no-look defense. Clark's team garnered the victory. Both teams hugged and high-fived and surrounded Clark at center court for photo-ops.

There is a common theme and prevailing attitude among Clark's men. The unity of purpose they all seemly share is to pursue and achieve high standards of education and facilitate the community with compassionate service.

Robert Byrd, a Chicago Bulls 1980 draft pick gave up his dream of playing professional basketball after leaving the team in Helsinki Finland to teach golf and life skills to underserved children at his *Bridging the Gap Learning Center Inc.* in Milwaukee, Wisconsin. Byrd says, "I want to provide an educational experience so rich that every child who passes through my door will be prepared to succeed, to follow his or her dream, and give back to the community in his or her own way."

In 2002, Washington D.C. Assistant Chief of Police Brian Jordan initiated the Youth Advisory Council (YAC) as a process to include area youth in community policing and problem solving. His department's objective is to partner these youth with a D.C. workforce who had similar upbringings and offer them better career choices.

The reports of what these former Jr. Trotters have done for their communities could go on and on, but like all good stories, there is an ending, and this ending will conclude with the comments of the Assistant Police Chief of Whittier California:

In California, as an adult I have coached basketball at the local YMCA, for Parks and Rec, and at various schools. About eight years ago when I was a Commander of the Headquarters Patrol Station, I remember walking in the employee hallway of the Sheriff's Department and I saw a 6'5 deputy that I did not recognize walking towards me. I thought to myself "I wonder if this guy can play ball," when he said "Hey coach!" I took a good look at him and then recognized that he was one of my former players that I had coached when I was a Deputy and he was 12 years old. He thanked me for working with him as a kid and for being a positive role model.

For me, Michael Clark was a flame of hope that burned bright in the darkness of poverty on the Southside of Chicago. But like the flame from any fire, the flame becomes its brightest when it touches something else and a new flame is created. Because Clark's flame touched my life in a positive way, it helped me master the life skills necessary not only to become successful personally, but it also allowed me to create flames of hope in other young people's lives as well. So I saw this weekend as an opportunity to tell Clark "Thank you for caring, being a positive role model, and teaching me how to make my flame burn brighter by touching others."

Kenton "Tiger" Rainey

Thank you Michael Clark for raising these Jr. Trotters from boys to men.

Copyright: Tony Brooks 2006

In 1976 Morgan Park and Levi Cobb returned to win the city championship after losing in 1975 in the city title game to Phillips. It was their 3rd straight year in the city title game. Coach Bill Warden deserved a lot of credit and he benefited from it by taking another position eventually.

This team squeaked by Dunbar(who they had defeated in

the final four the previous year) after trailing the whole game in the quarterfinal by 1 point as Jeff Barry stole the ball from Lester on an obvious reach-around-foul while the referees swallowed the whistle, and Ken Dancy's (left hand automatic as he was dubbed) last second shot rimmed out at the buzzer.

After winning the city, the magic carpet ride continued for Morgan Park as Laird Smith hit a jumper at the buzzer to beat Proviso West for the State championship. Levi Cobb, Jeff Barry, Laird Smith, and ended their career on a high note. They all had great careers and they had to be the luckiest team I have ever known. Maybe it was the rabbit's foot they said Cobb carried that I've referred to throughout this review. Still, they have my respect, big time.

While attending my 30th year high school reunion this year I had a conversation with Homer Lyons. He was a high school teammate who I had played organized basketball against prior to High school when we were 11 years old in the citywide biddy basketball league. He played for Fosco Park, and I played for Williams Park and the Magicians at that time.

While we complimented the men who kept kids busy playing organized ball in our inner city communities at Old Town, Dr. M.L. King, and Woodlawn Boys Clubs, as well as at Chatham YMCA, Homer mentioned that his potential might have never been maximized.

His beef was that he felt that he could've done so much more if he had been given more of an opportunity. He was a starter on our team that lost to the eventual state champion Morgan Park team that year. *By the way, rumor has it that a Key Morgan Park player constantly rubbed the lucky rabbit's foot they said he wore in his jock strap.*

That explains the luck they had while securing the one point victory against us in 1976.

I agreed with Homer, because I have always felt I could've done more also. What player doesn't look back and feel that he could've done more? That is why it is so important to let it all hang out while you are in the moment. You never want to look back and have regrets. I let Homer know that he was ahead of his time. He had the flashy game with the no look passes, the behind the back, and between the legs dribbling back then. He also had a smooth jump shot, but he was pulled quickly when he made mistakes using his flair and style. Even though Homer was fundamentally sound, I just feel that the coaching staff was not tolerant of, or ready for that style at that time. Home-boy, as he was dubbed was definitely ahead of his time.

He understood that he had to adapt his Westside style to the team's system, but the system was not ready to allow players to be flashy. We were really and truly taught to play basic basketball at that time. If he was playing today, he'd be looked at as one of the best. He was a 6'2" version of Magic Johnson from a ball handling and passing standpoint. I guess a message I can send to young basketball players using this example is to say: "In order to maximize your potential to the fullest extent, do everything exactly as the coach wants it to be done. If you do this, you will find that the coach will give you the freedom to insert your own creativity at certain parts of the game."

Both of us agreed that with minor adjustments we would've probably been the state champions in our senior year. Every former teammate I have spoken with has never forgotten the one point quarterfinal loss, or the 500 fans who waited and applauded as we returned to the school that night. It was our last high school game. Ah sports, the memories last a lifetime.

In 1977 Mark Aguirre, Eddie Johnson, Bernard Randolph and Skip Dillard were defeated by Phillips in the city championship game by Bernard Jackson, Sherrod Arnold, William Smith, Darius Clemmons, Carl Golston, Louis (Thief, 5 steals a game) Reymond, and Steve Parham. Tyrone Bradley was a budding star at this time. What a thief Louie Reymond was, and what a physical player who knew how to get away with it. I still have scratches from playing against him 30 years later.

St. Anselms gym was another 1970s place where the best of the best would play in the summertime. You could see the known and the unknown performing at the highest level here on any given night. The scouts would be here on occasion,

(Shelly Stark leading the pack) Even NBA coaches would come out to see. Many players were signed to European and pro contracts based on their performances at St. Anselm as well as at Chicago State, Washington Park, Malcolm X, and Dr. King Boys club. These guys I'm about to mention played at all locations around the city including the Pro/AM league held on the south Side at Washington Park on 55th street at King Drive. Prize money was always at stake, along with a trip to Boston to play in the national Pro/AM Invitational. The "Ravens", "Coca Cola", "Breyer's Hats", and "Real Nice" were some of the teams that played back in the day of the explosion of the Pro Am league to the basketball scene in the city.   Many of these players probably made all city or all section, but a only a select few went to the big time, but they all could dunk, shoot, run the floor and handle the ball with the best of them. Bill Rapier, the 6'5" star who never played in high school, but became an All American at Augustana College in Illinois, Gerard Campbell, the shooter from Englewood, along with Rennie Kelly who went to UCLA, Chester and Ronnie Giles of King, Efrem Winters, Teddy Grubbs, Kenny Curb, Snake Davis, Carl Nicks who played in the final four with Larry Bird at Indiana State, Stephon Butler, Nezzie Hurst, Craig Brittnum, Paul "Smooth" Vinson, Jeff Smith, Tim and Bud Nolden, Calvin Davis, Nate Strickland, Skip "Money" Dillard, Luther Rivers, Max Artis, Shane Price,

Ray Rhone, Lamone Lampley, Eddie Hughes, Eddie White, Henry Deaderick, Percy Leonard, Clyde King and Kenny Arnold from Calumet, Homer "Homeboy" Lyons, the Drinkard brothers from Cregier, Fred "Flip" Shepard, Marvin White, Darryl Sigh, Leonardo Drake, Zeke Rand, Darron Brittman, Paul Sidney, Arthur Bright, George White, Captain Video, and Chicago State All Americans Ken Dancy, Sherrod Arnold, Tank Eversley, and Terry Bradley. Keith Woolfolk, Keith Anderson, Calvin Young, Clifford Allen, Mark Lowry, Modzell Greer, Keith French, Michael Poole, (probably the second best 5'6" player ever, Sam Puckett is the best, while both of them averaged nearly 30 points per game) Andre Battle, Scoring Machine Len Williams from Harrison High who averaged 30 points per game as coach Ted Williams unleashed him game after game, and his brother, the physical Greg Williams of Loyola, who was drafted by the Dallas Cowboys for football even though he didn't play football in college. I played against Greg in the Pro/Am when he played for the Ravens. Boy was I sore from the physical play. There was also the Gray Family: Walter, Darryl, Dwayne, and Reno Gray from Hales. When you talk about basketball families, you have to mention the Irvin family. They have had 5 brothers (Lance, Mike, Mac, Nick, and Byron) who all played at the most competitive high school level, major college, and/or the professional levels. Their dad Mac Sr. is a neighborhood basketball legend, is also known around the city for his ability to put up big numbers. This is only the surface of the many players who performed at St. Anselm, Washington Park, Dr. King, IIT, Malcolm X College or Chicago State on one of those Hot Sunday Evenings. I know I missed some players who were top notch performers in the city, but I'll make sure we include all omissions in volume II of Inner City Hoops.

There are so many players who only played on the playground, but had big time skills.

So many factors go into making the pros. Not only do you have to be good, a number of things have to fall into place for you. For example: You have to be able to maintain a passing grade point average, not only in college, but at every level, Grade school, high school, and college as well. Many great players didn't make it because of grades. The next thing that has stopped a lot of great players from going pro is being in the right situation. If you wind up in a situation where you cannot do the things you do best, your full abilities are never showcased and you'll never be seen as a player who can play in the NBA. A lot of times you may need to consider transferring to a different situation, especially if you're a college player. Mike McKinney, a Penn University teammate of mine transferred 4 times while in college and became an all American who secured a European League contract as a senior at his 5th school. The main thing that will hold a player back is his inability to adapt his game to the coaches system. I have seen shooters, dunkers, and some of the greatest ball handlers fall by the wayside because they could not adapt their talents to the system of the coach. Most of the time it comes down to the basic fundamentals. If you learn the proper fundamentals of basketball, you should be able to adapt to any system and integrate your skills into the system. There have been players with all the individual skills who could not make it big because of inability to adapt to organized ball.

Of course we know that drugs and negative environmental forces of the inner city are also major reasons why many great players did not play at the next level. Everyone likes a talented athlete, so many times you can get caught up by socializing with the wrong crowd and it can cost you a career. One thing players should always remember is that a college education means a professional position in the workforce which can make your life a very productive one. I am speaking from the experience of going from inner city basketball player, to college, to the workforce as a degreed professional. There are so many with the same background in sports that have taken advantage. As a matter of fact, many of the names mentioned here are degreed professionals who are working in education, and many other capacities around the Chicago area. To some readers, it is probably surprising to you that the men I've mentioned here were such elite players. Many talk about how great they were, and many never talk about their careers. For example: Billy "the kid" Harris tells everyone he was the greatest, and he definitely was one of the best, who never had the opportunity to go to the big time, even though he played in the old American Basketball Association for the San Diego Conquistadores after the Chicago Bulls released him. On the other hand, no one would ever know that Educator Bill Saxton of Parker High was a leading scorer in the city during the 60s. He is by far one of the most humble high scorers I've ever known, along with Ronnie Lester, the former Chicago Bull and now assistant general manager in charge of scouting for the Los Angeles Lakers. History is wonderful, and that is the reason for this publication. Its just very fulfilling to know how everything around basketball has evolved to reach the point at which it is today.

In 1978 the Westinghouse crew returned to take the city. Eddie Johnson was gone, but the house had enough fire power with Aguirre, Dillard, and Randolph. They rolled over Manley and Russell Cross and Tim Anderson by defeating them by a small margin.

Russell Cross and Tim Anderson came back to the city championship game 2 more times,(79 and 80) winning it both times including the state championship in 1980. The 6'10" Cross was the dominant force, but Anderson was the steadying force, and Little-John Ellis who never got the credit was an excellent point guard who put the ball in the right places. They would say he was "shakin and bakin cake" Willie Little pulled the strings and got his due for coaching excellence.

There were 2 more state champions from Chicago in the 80s. Simeon won it in 84 with the outstanding play of Ben Wilson who was the number 1 player in the nation. At 6'8" he could do it all. He was a real treat to watch while flourishing in the Bob Hambric system of go to guys. Bobby Tribble was the shooter on the wing Rodney Hull was the rebounder/shot blocker, and Tim Bankston handled the ball with the best of them as he orchestrated the disciplined Simeon system. Hambric unleashed Bankston in the title game, and he was unstoppable as he showcased all of his skills. He could spin to the basket and score at will as he mystified the defense in that state championship game.

CHAPTER 11

THE 1980'S AND 1990'S

King High School Hall of Fame Coach Landon "Sonny" Cox emerged as a mainstay in the city championship game in the 80s. he won state championships in 86, 90, and 93. He has appeared in 10 city championship games and has won 6 of them.(86,87,89,90,93,and 99) He has the highest winning percentage of any coach in the history of the IHSA. What can you say about Sonny except that he is a winner. He has coached a huge number of outstanding players: Marcus Liberty, Levertis Robertson, Leon Smith, Jamie Brandon (all time leading scorer in the history of the public league), Johhny Selvie, Ahmad Sharif, Anthony Johnson, Imari Sawyer, Efrem Winters, Teddy Grubbs, Fred Sculfield and many more. The list is endless.

Farragut won the city title in 1995 with Kevin Garnett, Michael Wright, and Ronnie Fields, but lost to Thornton at the state. That is puzzling, but we know the favorite doesn't always come in, but nobody would have bet against Kevin Garnett and super leaper Fields that year.

Leaper Tai Streets, Son of playground player, Dunbar's Clayton Streets made the difference for Thornton. He went on to Michigan University, and now plays wide out in the NFL, and sponsors a local AAU team called Mean Streets.

The only Chicago team other than King to win a state title in the 90s is the Whitney Young Dolphins. The dolphins are currently the last team from Chicago to win a state championship in the 90's. They were coached by another hall of fame member, George Stanton. A strong disciplinarian and excellent fundamental teacher, Stanton took a group of talented players and molded them into a team. You would not see a more disciplined team who could play any style of basketball. They could run and shoot, or they could slow it down. They had size and speed. Quentin Richardson, the leader made their second consecutive trip to the state tournament a charm. He is certainly one of the best ever. His supporting cast included Dennis Gates who was the defender who could also score and Cordell Henry, a quick masterful ball handler who distributed it wisely along with Freshman future all state selection, Najeeb Echols who gave great support off the bench.

It is surprising to many that only 14 state championships have been won by Chicago, and it has been debated forever that more than 1 of our 100 high school teams should be allowed to qualify for the state tourney. Chicago Public Schools CEO Arne Duncan, an outstanding player in his own right brought about the elimination of the automatic bid to the city champion in 2003, and the Chicago Public League has since been divided into a two class system during state play. It actually has created more opportunities for all schools because, instead of just the city champion, every Chicago team plays in the state tourney. Also, small schools get the chance to play against schools their own size during state tournament play. On three occasions since the elimination of the automatic bid there has been more than one team from Chicago making it to elite eight which is played at the state tournament. Two of those occasions have included class AA teams which are large schools. Our teams finished first and third in 2006, and would've been first and second if they were not bracketed in such a way that they had to meet and eliminate each other. Elimination of one prior to the state championship was inevitable. Two CPS teams have never met for the state championship, but I believe that it will happen in the near future. A number of coaches wanted to keep an automatic berth for the city champion. They feel that winning the city title is worth an automatic bid to the elite eight. I can't disagree because one thing for sure is that no league is tougher than the one hundred (100) plus teams that make up the Chicago Public League. To win the city is a huge achievement. Winning the state championship is icing on the cake. Many teams have fallen victim to a let down after winning the city championship. Eliminating the automatic bid to the state tourney for winning the city title has been somewhat controversial, but it has truly created opportunities for teams to experience playing in the state tourney, and a second chance to qualify for the state championship. I must say that no team state wide has to travel the road that a public league team travels. It's tough to win the city, but I've always felt that if you win the city championship, you have an excellent chance of winning the state title as well. Even if you need to play your way through the state playoffs after you've won the city championship.

CHAPTER 12

HOW CITY TEAMS FARED AT THE
STATE TOURNEY SINCE 1950

H ere are the state tournament results for Chicago's city championship teams since 1950. Take a look at how they faired in the state tourney after winning the city title:

1950

Tilden won in the first round over Sterling 46-35, but lost in the second round to Elgin 59-50.

1951

Parker High was defeated in the first round by Robinson High

1952

Chicago Roosevelt lost in the first round to Pickneyville 56-44.

1953

Du Sable High was defeated in the first round by LaGrange 85-68.

1954

Du Sable returned with future Globe Trotter Paxton Lumpkin, and "Sweet" Charlie Brown to defeat Bowen , Quincy and Edwardsville before bowing to Mount Vernon in the title game 76-70

1955

Chicago's Marshall High is defeated by Quincy in the first round 70-59.

1956

Dunbar defeats Winnetka, and Rantoul before losing in the semi finals to Rockford West 61-48. They returned the same night and won the third place game over Oak Park River Forest High 73-56.

1957

Crane loses to Evanston in the first round 67-60.

1958

Chicago Marshall wins Chicago's first state Championship right before I was born by defeating Rock Falls in the state title game 70-64. They beat Elgin 63-43, Herrin 72-59, and Aurora West 74-62 to get to the title game.

1959

Marshall returns and loses in the first round to Waukegan 63-62.

1960

Marshall wins it all again defeating Elgin 71-55, Monmouth 55-35, Decatur 74-62, and Bridgeport 79-55 to win the title game.

1961

Marshall takes third place after defeating Peoria Manual 73-58 which soothes their semi final loss to Harvey Thornton 49-47.

1962

Carver makes it all the way to the title game before succumbing 49-48 to Decatur.

They defeated St Patrick 48-42, Centralia 56-50, and Mcleansboro 54-41 on the way to the title game.

1963

Carver wins the state championship by defeating Centralia in a great game 53-52.

1964

Crane loses in two overtimes in the first round to Evanston 55-53.

1965

Marshall takes 3rd place by defeating Harvey 66-59 after losing to Collinsville 76-74 in the semi final round. They had earlier victories over Winnetka,69-52, and Moline 75-72.

1966

Winnetka defeated Marshall in the first round 78-60.

1967

Harlan loses in the first round to Elmhurst in a 72-70 squeaker.

1968

Crane defeats Lagrange 73-61, then Carbondale in overtime 64-63, then lose in the semi final round to Evanston 70-54. They come back and defeat Dekalb in the third place game 82-62.

1969

Hirsch loses in the first round by a point to Proviso East 47-46.

1970

Harlan is defeated in the first round 68-61

1971

Harlan loses again in the first round to Thorn ridge, the eventual state champion 73-63.

1972

Super sectional format begins and city champ advances to the state quarterfinal after the city title game. Crane loses to Quincy in the Quarterfinals 87-71

1973

Hirsch wins the state title, the first of the 70s, by beating Winnetka's New Truer East for the championship 65-51. Along the way they beat Moline 57-50, and Lockport central 83-67.

1974

A young Morgan Park team loses to Proviso east 75-55 in the quarter finals.

1975

The Phillips Wildcats return and win the state title. They defeat Waukegan 67-61, Peoria Richwoods 86-69, and Bloom 76-48 for the championship.

1976

The same group of Morgan Park Mustangs (from 1974) return and win the state championship on a last second shot beating Aurora West 45-44. Other victories were 53-48 over Gales burg and 59-58 over Oak Park. (There's a rumor that a key Morgan Park player carried a lucky rabbit's foot) They said the toughest team they played was Dunbar during their run.

1977

Phillips loses in the quarter finals 56-50 to ST Laurence catholic.

1978

Isiah Thomas and St. Joseph defeat Westinghouse in the Quarter finals 63-60.

1979

Quincy defeats Chicago Manley 75-63 in the quarterfinals.

1980

Manley wins the state championship by defeating Downers Grove South 55-54, Lincoln 59-45, and Effingham 69-61 for the championship.

1981

Westinghouse loses in the semifinals to proviso east 72-66, and settle for third place by defeating Wheaton Central 53-47. They also defeated New Truer East 62-60 in the quarter finals.

1982

Marshall gets fourth place after defeating St. Joseph 79-59, and losing one to East St. Louis Lincoln 57-54, and one to Quincy 62-61

1983

Marshall gets fourth place again by defeating Elgin 59-46, but losing to Peoria 58-57, and to Thornton 65-60.

1984

Simeon wins it's first state title defeating Evanston 53-47. They also conquered Rock Island 48-44, and Aurora West 67-58.

1985

Simeon loses to Springfield Lumpier, 52-48.

1986

King defeats Rich Central for the title 47-40 after defeating Evanston Township 64-62, and Peoria Manual 79-62.

1987

King loses in the title game to east St. Louis 79-62. King defeated Elgin 70-58, and St. Joseph 60-58 to get there.

1988

Simeon goes down in overtime to St. Francis De Sales 60-57.

1989

King takes third place beating Rock Island 70—58. They lost to east St. Louis 60-57, after beating Thorn ridge 53-46 in the quarterfinals.

1990

King High beats Gordon tech catholic for the championship 65-55. Along the way King defeated East St. Louis Lincoln 60-49, and Aurora West 66-58.

1991

Marshall takes third place beating Libertyville 67-65 to come back from their semi final loss to Peoria Manual 68-55. They had defeated Batavia 56-46 earlier in the quarter finals.

1992

Westinghouse gets third place winning 96-69 over Rockford Moylan after losing 64-47 to Proviso East in the semi finals. They defeated Aurora east earlier in the quarter finals 63-42.

1993

King reigns again after beating Rockford Guilford 79-42 in the title game. They beat Danville 69-38, and Proviso East 82-54 as they dominated everyone.

1994

Westinghouse loses in the quarterfinals to Peoria Manual 81-76.

1995

Farragut (with Kevin Garnett, Michael Wright, and Ronnie Fields)loses in the quarter finals to Thornton 46-43

1996

Westinghouse takes third place beating New Truer 60-58 after falling to Thornton 69-54. The house squeaked by Hoffman Estates 42-41 in the quarter finals.

1997

Whitney Young is defeated by Peoria Manual in the quarterfinals 51-46.

1998

Whitney Young returns and runs through the field to the title by defeating Elgin 68-50, Quincy 62-34, and Galesburg 61-56 for the championship.

1999

King wins the third place game over Schamburg 67-58 after losing in the semifinals to St. Joseph 59-40.

2000

Westinghouse takes second place after losing in the title game to West Aurora.

2001

Morgan Park loses in the semifinal round to Eddie Curry and Thornwood, but rebounds to take third place

2002

Westinghouse wins the state championship by defeating Springfield

2003

VonSteuben loses in the quarterfinal round at the hands of Peoria in the first year that the automatic bid was eliminated. They earned their way to the state quarterfinals even though they were not the city champ.

2004

Farragut and Simeon make the elite eight, but both teams lose in the first round. Neither team was the city champ but benefited from the new format.

2005

Crane and Sherron Collins lose to Carbondale in the first round of the quarterfinals at the state tourney after again being a team who advanced without winning the city title.

2006

Derrick Rose makes a dramatic buzzer shot in overtime to defeat the hometown Peoria team and win the state title for the Simeon Wolverines after a steal of the inbound pass by Dexter Williams to become the first city champion since the removal of the automatic bid to win the state championship.

CHAPTER 13

STATE CHAMPIONS SINCE 1950

N ow let us take a look at the state champions since 1950. It is interesting to see what parts of the state has won the most state championships at the high school level even though Chicago has sent the most players to the NBA. Here is the list of state champions:

1950

Mount Vernon

1951

Freeport

1952

Hebron

1953

LaGrange

1954

Mount Vernon

1955

Rockford West

1956

Rockford West

1957

Herrin

1958

Chicago Marshall

1959

Springfield

1960

Chicago Marshall

1961

Collinsville

1962

Decatur

1963

Chicago Carver

1964

Pekin

1965

Collinsville

1966

Thornton Harvey

1967

Pekin

1968

Evanston Township

1969

Proviso East- Maywood

1970

LaGrange

1971

Thornridge

1972

Thornridge

1973

Chicago Hirsch

1974

Proviso East-Maywood

1975

Chicago Phillips

1976

Chicago Morgan Park

1977

Peoria

1978

Lockport Central

1979

Maine South-Park Ridge

1980

Chicago Manley

1981

Quincy

1982

East St. Louis Lincoln

1983

Springfield Lumpier

1984

Chicago Simeon

1985

Chicago Mount Carmel Catholic

1986

Chicago King

1987

East St, Louis Lincoln

1988

East St. Louis Lincoln

1989

East St. Louis Lincoln

1990

Chicago King

1991

Proviso East-Maywood

1992

Proviso east-Maywood

1993

Chicago King

1994

Peoria Manual

1995

Peoria Manual

1996

Peoria Manual

1997

Peoria Manual

1998

Chicago Whitney Young

1999

St. Joseph-Westchester

2000

West Aurora

2001

Schaumburg beats Thornwod and Curry

2002

Westinghouse defeats Springfield as Darius Glover takes control, and sophomore Jamarcus "Tom-Tom" Ellis comes of age

2003

Peoria wins the state title

2004

Peoria Central takes the title behind the leadership of Shawn Livingston

2005

Glenbrook North and Jon Scheyer win the state

2006

Simeon prevails as junior guard Derrick Rose's buzzer shot in overtime after Dexter Williams' steal broke the hearts of the home town Peoria team that night. It was exciting to witness as I sat next to Chicago Public Schools CEO Arne Duncan and celebrated with him. Rose proved that he is a true blue chipper.

CHAPTER 14

THE CHICAGO PUBLIC SCHOOL'S NBA PLAYERS

Nat "Sweet Water" Clifton	Minneapolis Lakers
Lonnie Lynn	Minneapolis Lakers
Johnny "Red" Kerr	Minneapolis Lakers
Cazzie Russell	New York Knicks
Tim Hardaway	Golden State
Kenny Miller	GoldenState
Kelvin Upshaw	Celtics
Sonny Parker	Celtics
Rickey Green	Celtics
Kevin Porter	Detroit
Chris Harris	Detroit
Maurice Cheeks	76ers
Mark Aguirre	Dallas
Eddie Johnson	Phoenix
Leon Smith	Dallas
Terry Cummings	Clippers
Robert Byrd	Milwaukee

Rashard Griffin	Milwaukee
Bo Ellis	Denver
Kiwane Garris	Denver
Kevin Garnett	Wolves
Walter Bond	Wolves
Marlon Maxey	Wolves
George Wilson	Royals
Emmet Bryant	Royals
Ken Dancy	Washington
Alfredrick Hughes	San Antonio
Eddie Hughes	Utah
Tony Brown	Utah
Jeff Wilkins	Utah
Sherrod Arnold	Dallas
Byron Irvin	Blazers
Cliff Meely	Blazers
Gregory Parham	Milwaukee
Ken Norman	Clippers
Quentin Richardson	Clippers
Hersey Hawkins	Seattle
Ronnie Lester	Bulls
Randy Brown	Bulls
Billy Harris	Bulls
Carl Nicks	Utah
Larry Lewis	Philadelphia

Rashard Griffith	Milwaukee
Mitchell JJ Anderson	Utah
Andre Wakefield	Bulls/Detroit
Modzell Greer	Indiana
Keith French	Phoenix
Tom Hawkins	Royals
Tyrone Addams	Royals
Mickey Johnson	Bulls
Darius Clemmons	Bulls
Larry Williams	Denver
Darius Clemmons	Bulls
Marcus Liberty	Dallas
Priest Lauderdale	Atlanta
Thomas Hamilton	Houston
Nick Anderson	Orlando
Troy Hudson	Clippers
Voise Winters	Philadelphia
Keith French	Phoenix Suns
Mark Lowry	Detroit Pistons
Nazi Mohammed	Philadelphia
Larry Lewis	Philadelphia
AlFredrick Hughes	San Antonio
Bill Robinzine	Kansas City
Eddie Johnson	Phoenix
Hersey Hawkins	Charlotte

Mark Aguirre	Dallas
Kiwane Garris	Denver
Juwaan Howard	Washington
Darryl "Sky" Walker	Washington/Chicago/Los Angeles
Tony Allen	Boston
Will Bynum	Boston
Dwayne Wade	Miami
Bobby Simmons	Milwaukee

CHAPTER 15

STATE CHAMPIONSHIP COACHES FROM CHICAGO

Interestingly enough there have only been eleven (11) Chicago Public League coaches Who have won the 14 state championships in Illinois history. Considering the number of public league players who have made it professionally, you would think that there would be more state titles, even though 14 is more than 20 percent since 1950. The most ironic statistic is that even though two of our coaches won multiple state titles, none of our coaches have ever won back to back state championship titles. I already know that that statistic could change this year as Simeon is one of the favorites to win a state title in 2007. A state title would place coach Robert Smith in the history books as the only public league coach to win consecutive state championships.

Well, here are the Elite State Championship Coaches:

Landon "Sonny" Cox, Martin Luther King High School

Who else should be listed first? There's no question that coach Cox, who has amazingly won three (3) of the 14 state titles that the Chicago Public Schools have claimed should be listed first. This coach has won six (6) city titles and made (ten) 10 city championship appearances. Through hard work and dedication, he has built a dynasty at King High School. A number of his players have gone on to the NBA. Marcus Liberty, Rashard Griffin, Thomas Hamilton, and Jamie Brandon are a few who have played professionally, as well as Leon Smith, who was drafted out of high school. This writer feels that Coach Cox has certainly shown that he knows what to do to win. In all six appearances at the state finals, he never left without taking home a trophy, which he did each time he appeared. The key to his success in my opinion was the fact that he let the players do what they did best. He unleashed them. If you were a rebounder, you had to rebound. If you were a scorer, you were allowed to score. The phenomenal success of coach Cox separates him from his peers. He has the highest winning percentage in the history of the Illinois High School Association. Enough Said! This multi-talented gentleman doesn't play a bad saxophone either. If you've never heard "High Heel Sneakers", or "Walk On By", you should go out and get the CD.

Isadore"Spin" Salario, John Marshall High School

This John Marshall High School coach won two (2) state titles including the first Chicago Public Schools state title in 1959 with George Wilson. He returned again two years later and won it again. He put together the most dominant team during the late fifties and early 60s. He is remembered for his fast break style of offense.

Larry Hawkins, Carver High School

Larry Hawkins is one of the most respected basketball personalities in Chicago basketball history. I will refer to him as Larry "Legend." He took his Carver challengers to the state championship "game" in consecutive seasons. He lost the title game by one point in 1962, but returned to take the title back to Chicago in 1963 as he defeated Centralia by one point. Cazzie Russell, a future star at Michigan and NBA number one draft pick to be, was the most outstanding player on the 1962 team and became a future overall number one draft pick.

Charles Stimpson, Hirsch High School

This team played pressure defense, and ran the floor like no team before them. Future NBA star Ricky Green has to be the fastest point guard in CPS history. Robert Brooks, Joshua Smith and John Robinson stepped up big time at the state tourney. Stimpson let them play and show their natural talents and playground skills. That was the key to his success. Rickey Green went on to star at Michigan and in the NBA.

Herb Brown, Wendell Phillips High School

Coach Brown's team pressured the ball and ran even faster than Hirsch to win the state title. Coach Brown believed in pressure, pressure, and more pressure. When he had the lead in the fourth quarter, it was all over because he went to the four corners and made opponents foul.

He knew how to feed his big man and had shooters to keep defenses honest. In 1975 their pressure defense and Larry Williams on offense made the difference.

Bill Warden, Morgan Park High School

Coach Warden and his Mustang crew was a huge force in the mid 70s. They appeared in the state tourney twice in 3 years, winning it all once in 1976. He also led them to 3 city championship games. His Levi Cobb led teams were very effective for all 4 years.

Willie Little, Manley High School

The late Coach Willie Little used the inside – outside game to perfection with future Purdue University star Russell Cross as the post man, Tim Anderson on the wing, and Little John Ellis in the role of distributor. This group played the *inside -*

outside - penetration style of basketball to perfection. I respect coach Little's knowledge of what it takes to win. He's a good fit as a member of this elite group of coaches.

Bob Hambric, Simeon High School

Legend has it that Bob Hambric, as a player never saw a shot he didn't take. As a coach, his philosophy is one of extreme discipline. His state title is especially memorable because it was the first city team to get credit for being disciplined. They could run, dunk, and shoot long jumpers, but they could also slow it down and run plays that looked like road maps with many screens in between. The late All America Player Ben Wilson, Bobby Tribble, and Tim Bankston were the keys on this 1984 state championship team.

George Stanton, Whitney Young High School

George Stanton was riding the waves of his second consecutive trip down state, which was a charm. Here is another coach who knows how to put it all together to win. His philosophy is a combination of all of the best coaching techniques including there is no I in team. He had a team with all parts working together. This group was able to play any style of basketball. They could run, run set plays in a controlled offense, play tough pressure man to man defense, turn on the crowd with slam dunk highlights, feature an individual player as a go to guy, or sit on the ball to close out an opponent. Quentin Richardson was the given scoring leader, but this team also featured a defender, a ball handler, a rebounder, and any of four players who could pick up the slack and score on a given day. The kids followed the leadership of coach Stanton, overcame all opponents, and won it all in 1998.

Chris Head, Westinghouse High School

Christopher Head is one of the most fiery coaches who ever coached in the public league. He is also an excellent teacher of fundamental basketball. After coming up short two years earlier, his team, which was undersized, defeated teams who were rated higher all along the way. Senior captain Darius Glover led the team, while the blossoming sophomore Jamarcus Ellis showed glimpses of his outstanding talents. They defeated a very good Springfield team that was led by Andre Iguodala who now plays for the Philadelphia 76ers.

Robert Smith, Simeon High School

What an exciting championship season we witnessed in 2006. The Simeon Wolverines and Derick Rose warmed up for their state title run by putting on a great show at the United Center during the Public League championship game. Along the way to the title, they faced a number of tough challenges from Proviso East, Glenbrook North, and others. Marshall, who was the 3rd place state finisher, and an additional public league school to make it to the elite eight in 2006 showed the public league dominance in basketball, but this is Simeon and Robert Smith's space so let me tell you how exciting their championship run was. In the first state quarterfinal game they met number one ranked Glenbrook North and defeated them soundly as Dexter Williams shut down John Scheyer while playing the role of stopper in the box and one defense. It was a strategy that Robert Smith used effectively throughout the season. Next they had to defeat Marshall, who had beaten them earlier in the season. It was a tough battle but Simeon prevailed. In the championship game the wolverines silenced the home town crowd of 10,000 as Rose made a driving shot in the lane at the buzzer after Dexter Williams stole the inbound pass in overtime. The small Chicago crowd erupted and stormed the floor. I sat with CEO Arne Duncan, and Chief Officer Don Pittman who enjoyed this victory thoroughly. Coach Robert Smith has set the table to become the only coach in the history of the public league to win consecutive state titles. He has a good number of his key players returning, including superstar Derrick Rose who is ranked among the top 5 high school players in the country. From what I've observed I believe he is number one because of his all around skill level, and his unselfish play. He only takes over a game when he needs to, and he seems to enjoy setting the table for others.

ABOUT THE AUTHOR

Calvin Davis resides in the Beverly area in the city of Chicago. He is the Director of the Chicago Public Schools High School and Elementary School Citywide Athletic Programs and Sports Facilities. Calvin is also the Supervisor for the Citywide Driver Education Program, and works closely with the Physical Education Curriculum program as well. His family lived at 32nd and Prairie Avenue for 22 years. This product of the Chicago school system attended Douglas Elementary School for grades kindergarten through eight, and Dunbar Vocational High School for grades 9 through twelve. He was naturally a very gifted baseball player, but his love for basketball started in the sixth grade when he tried out for the Magicians Citywide Biddy basketball team. That team was coached by Michael Clark and later became known as the Jr. Trotters, and was probably one of the first versions of an AAU traveling program. The Harlem Globetrotters sponsored that team. Calvin played with this group from 1969 through 1975 as one of the original Jr. Trotters. He played on the Douglas All Stars 8th grade City Championship team in 1972. He also graduated as the class Valedictorian with honors for every subject area and straight A's that same year. He went on to Dunbar Vocational High School where his teams won the sectional titles in his freshman and sophomore years. In his junior year, Dunbar went to the city's final four (semifinals) before losing at the Amphitheater. As a senior, Calvin played on a team that went to the quarter final round of the city's playoffs before losing to the eventual state champion, Morgan Park by one point. Calvin still talks about that loss today about the no-call by officials whose names I won't mention, and how Ken Dancy's buzzer shot rimmed out. After graduating with high honors, Calvin went to William Penn University for four years. He played as a 6'3" wing player, who earned all conference honors twice, was a member of a conference championship team once, and played in one NCAA Division III Western Regional playoff series. Calvin received his Bachelor of Arts Degree in Education, with History and Physical Education as the subjects he was certified to teach. After teaching and coaching in the Chicago Public Schools for a number of years between Beethoven Elementary School, and Du Sable High School, Calvin returned to school at Chicago State University and received his Master of Arts Degree in

Educational Administration and Supervision, with a Principal's endorsement and Certification in General Administration. He also received an award for outstanding Academic Achievement from Chicago State University as he compiled a 3.9 Grade Point Average on a scale of 4.0 in the graduate Studies Program. Calvin has played organized basketball as an adult in the 35 and over men's "prize money" league, and the 6'3" and under league, and still plays basketball recreationally between occasional rounds of golf. He is a basketball and sports fanatic who can explain and teach all of the technical, and physical aspects of basketball and other sports. He still professes to be a pure shooter who can still dunk a basketball at 48 years of age. He wanted to write this book because basketball has become so popular around the country, and it has meant so much to him. He hopes that this publication will touch some of the young people who read it, and have a positive influence on them as they participate in sports programs. His feeling is that it is exciting to learn about the history of how the game has grown in Chicago. He thought it would be nice if the young players could read about the history of the game in the inner city of Chicago. His feeling is that not only will this book be educational, but it will motivate and help youths to understand how to use basketball as a tool to help you along the path of success. Of course there are many who were not mentioned, and that is probably the greatest reason to write volume 2 of "Inner City Hoops", which illustrates why Chicago plays the best basketball. Since becoming director of Chicago Public League Sports, Calvin has conducted a study of the student information system in Chicago. In each of the past three years, the student-athletes have had higher attendance percentages, higher grade point averages, and higher graduation rates than the general student population. This fact just highlights the impact of sports and it's significance even more. Early academic success really drove Calvin to continue to achieve good grades. He was a straight E and A student for most of his school years. He is a member of 3 Hall of Fame classes: the Dunbar High School, Hall of Fame, the Illinois High School Association Basketball Hall of Fame, and the Chicago Public League Basketball Coaches Association Hall of Fame. One bit of advice he'd like to give to young people is to strive for academic success by working for good grades at an early age, because academic success is truly the key to a successful and productive life. Also, young people need to listen to the words of advice from their parents, and the adults who have previously had success with the experiences that a young person is currently planning for, or going through. Good listening skills will help contribute to a healthy, and successful life.

CHICAGO'S ALL TIME BEST PLAYERS, BY POSITION

Calvin's Choices

POINT GUARDS

NAME	SCHOOL
ISIAH THOMAS	ST JOSEPH
MAURICE CHEEKS	DUSABLE
GLENN RIVERS	PROVISO EAST
TIM HARDAWAY	CARVER
KEVIN PORTER	DUSABLE
RICKEY GREEN	HIRSCH
RONNIE LESTER	DUNBAR
SAM PUCKETT	HALES
CARL NICKS	ENGLEWOOD
PAXTON LUMPKIN	DUSABLE
RANDY BROWN	COLLINS
LLOYD WALTON	MOUNT CARMEL

Special Mention: Kelvin Upshaw, Reginald "Kato" King, Eddie Hughes, Kiwane Garris, Leon Hillard, Donald Whiteside, Cody Butler, Michael Poole, Arthur Sivels, Nick Irvin, Stephon Butler, Carl Golston, Sherrod Arnold, Paul Vinson, Al "Runt" Pullins, Jeff Stewart, Skip Dillard, Marty Murray, Sam Gowers, Stevie King, James Jackson. Tony Brown, Imari Sawyer, Nate Mason, Reynaldo Bryant, Arne Duncan, John Ellis, Jelani Boline, Clarence Notree, Robert Brooks, Vince "Dimp" Robinson, Darryl Gray, Dwayne Gray, Reno Gray, Percy Leonard, Greg Williams, Darryl Sigh, Richard "Doc" Byrd, Cyrus McGinnis, Phil "Slick" Harris, and Cordell Henry.

BEST WING GUARDS

NAME	SCHOOL
JAMIE BRANDON	KING
BILLY HARRIS	DUNBAR
HERSEY HAWKINS	WESTINGHOUSE
DARRYL WALKER	CORLISS
ANDRE WAKEFIELD	CRANE
LEN WILLIAMS	HARRISON
DARIUS CLEMONS	PHILLIPS
KENNY ARNOLD	CALUMET
RONNIE FIELDS	FARRAGUT
ANDRE BANKS	MENDEL
LEARTHUR SCOTT	GORDON TECH
AL "PEG" SAUNDERS	DUNBAR

Special Mention: Pierre Cunningham, Andre Battle, Bernard Jackson, Tim Bankston, Charlie Jones, Deon Butler, Bill Saxton, Ralph Dillard, Tyrone Bradley, Larry Harper, Rennie Kelly, Mitch Mosley, Bryant Notree, Ray Bullocks, Darryl Brown, Brooks Taylor, Tony McCoy, Tony Pruitt, Anthony Brown, Mac Irvin, and Bobby Tribble.

Extra Special Mention:

Calvin Davis: (a pure jumpshot, a top defender, a 37" vertical, and because he wrote this book)

BEST SMALL FORWARDS

NAME	SCHOOL
MARK AGUIRRE	WESTINGHOUSE
EDDIE JOHNSON	WESTINGHOUSE
SONNY PARKER	FARRAGUT
QUENTIN	WHITNEY YOUNG
RICHARDSON	KING
MARCUS LIBERTY	DUSABLE
CHARLIE BROWN	ROBESON
ALFREDRICK	METRO
HUGHES	CRANE
MITCHELL JJ	GAGE PARK
ANDERSON	LINDBLOM
KEN NORMAN	SIMEON
VOISE WINTERS	
MICKEY JOHNSON	
NICK ANDERSON	

Special Mention: Agis Bray, Robert Byrd, Bernard Mills, Sev-ira Brown, Arthur Bright, Ken Dancy, Walter Gray, Johnny B Williams, Shaky Jakes, Johnny Melvin, and Donnell Thomas Darryl Yancy, William McQuitter, Craig Robinson, Cedric Banks, Clifford Allen, Antonio "Snake" Flowers, Tony Harris, Don Russell, Jones Richmond, Rennie Kelly, Craig Bowman, George White, Fred "Flip" Shepard, Henry Tiggs, Eddie White, Laird Smith, Joshua Smith, and Nougie Watkins. .

BEST POWER FORWARDS

NAME	SCHOOL
TERRY CUMMINGS	CARVER
BENJI WILSON	SIMEON
ABE BOOKER	WELLS
EFREM WINTERS	KING
DAN DAVIS	CRANE
JOHNNY SELVIE	KING
RUFUS CALHOUN	BOWEN
DEON THOMAS	SIMEON
LEVERTIS ROBINSON	KING
RAY PRICE	DUNBAR
BILL ROBINZINE	PHILLIPS
LEVI COBB	MORGAN PARK

Special Mention: Bill Robinzine, Teddy Grubbs, Marcellous Starks, Lonnie Lynne, Wally West, Herman Hoskins, Keith Anderson, Keith Woolfolk, Kenny "Snake"Davis, and Bill Dise, Joe Stiffend, Sherwen Enforcer" Moore, Marvin White, Bill Rapier, Gregory Parham and Tank Eversley.

BEST CENTERS OF ALL TIME

NAME	SCHOOL
NAT "SWEETWATER"	DUSABLE
CLIFTON	PARKER (NOW
MAURICE "BO" ELLIS	ROBESON)
MEL DAVIS	DUNBAR
GEORGE WILSON	MARSHALL
LARRY WILLIAMS	PHILLIPS
RUSSELL CROSS	MANLEY
JOHN ROBINSON	HIRSCH
RASHARD GRIFFITH	KING
BILLY LEWIS	FARRAGUT
DONNIE VON MOORE	KENWOOD
LARRY "MOON	DUSABLE
COOKIE" LEWIS	KING
LEON SMITH	

Special Mention: Nazir Muhammed, Rodney Hull, Charles Brakes, Tommy Hamilton, Melvin McCants, John Fleming, Wally West, Larue Martin, George Montgomery, Mike Robinson and Leonardo Drake.

Honorary Coaches: Landon Cox, Isadore "Spin" Salario, Larry Hawkins, Herb Brown, George Stanton, Don Pittman, Charles Redmond, Chuck Frazier, Michael Clark, and Luther Bedford.

All Time Best Officials: Nate Humphreys, Richard Reels, Malcolm Hemphill, Reuben Norris, L.T. Bonner, and Mau Cason.

NATIONAL RECOGNITION
ARRIVES DURING THE 70S

As the years went by, colleges all over the country began to recruit players from the Chicago area. The late 70s was when recruiting really heated up. Basketball aficionados around the country realized the fact that Chicago had a huge pool of talent in their 75 high schools at that time. Today (in 2007) there are 128 high schools in Chicago.

Chicago's finest players were rated as just as good, if not better than east coast players from New York and Philadelphia. The scouts were coming out in droves. During this time, Chicago area products who would go on to stardom in the NBA were all starring at major universities in the Midwest. Some of them were Isaiah Thomas, Mark Aguirre, Eddie Johnson, Terry Cummings, and Glenn Rivers. Scholarship offers grew in large proportions during this time. It got to the point where you could average ten points per game on a good team, and receive a scholarship to a major university. When this happened, it confirmed the fact that

Chicago had become one of the top areas to recruit players with outstanding basketball talent. This was a sign of respect, because in the past, only the top stars who averaged 20 points per game or more were offered scholarships to major universities. This is why it is important that young players know about the past. They can learn the history of basketball, as well as the legacy of the players of the past who made opportunities what they are today. All of this occurred long before AAU became what it is known as today, because in today's high school basketball world, AAU really drives the ranking of players nationally. Evaluation camps are also a big stage for recognition today. Shootouts are another avenue for talent to be discovered in today's basketball communities. I really do believe that if not for the outstanding players of yesteryear who put Chicago on the map, opportunities that exist today might not be as plentiful as they are today. The players I'm speaking of brought respect and recognition for the talent that has always been in Chicago.

As I've shown in the 20,000 words in this publication, the nation has come to recognize that "Chicago's Inner City Hoops" Are among The Very Best.

The following Chicago Sun-Times Newspaper article "City Athletics Headed in Right Direction" written by prep sports writer Tina Akouris shows what I'm attempting to do today to impact athletics in the Chicago Public Schools High School Sports Program. As my favorite college professor Clarence Fitch would say, It's all about: "NEVERENDING IMPROVEMENT".

CITY ATHLETICS HEADED IN RIGHT DIRECTION

Tina Akouris

The president of the United States has a State of the Union address every winter. Calvin Davis, the director of sports administration for the Chicago Public League, should have a State of the Public League address each spring. As the 2005-06 school year winds down, Davis and the Public League can identify sports to be proud of and sports that need improvement.

HIGHLIGHTS AND LOWLIGHTS

Producing Division I college football recruits is one of Davis' biggest bragging rights. There were eight Division I signees from the Public League, including four from Morgan Park: Demetrius Jones (Notre Dame), Ramone Johnson (Tennessee), Chris James (Illinois) and Corbin Bryant (Northwestern). Hubbard became the second Public League football team in two years to advance to the state semifinals when the Greyhounds played Normal. They lost 34-6.

Another football highlight Davis is proud of was Morgan Park ending its season with a 14-13 overtime victory against Brother Rice in the Prep Bowl.

For those accomplishments, Davis credits the 10-year-old tackle- football program in city elementary schools for producing players who enter high school already having played the game.

"I think football is on the brink of breaking through," Davis said. "CPS football has never won a state championship, and right now we are on the brink of having a team win a state championship. There is stability in the program."

Football is on Davis' list of thriving Public League sports. That list also includes boys and girls basketball, boys soccer, baseball, bowling and girls track.

But he also has a list of sports that need improvement: boys track, cross-country, softball, volleyball, swimming, golf, tennis, water polo and wrestling.

Davis, who is in his third year as director of sports administration, said his criteria are based on how competitive the sports have been at the state level from a team perspective, not necessarily from an individual perspective.

And the sport Davis seems most concerned about is

wrestling.

"Wrestling really needs support," Davis said. "They need strong leadership because they do have committed people. We need to get more kids involved and get football players to be members of the wrestling team."

Davis said he is willing to provide more coaching and resources and upgraded equipment to improve wrestling.

There seems to be agreement that one of the solutions to improving boys track and cross-country is participation at the elementary school level.

Mather senior Ahsan Khan runs cross-country and track. Khan said that when he started running during his freshman year, it took him about two months to get used to cross-country. But if a school can get a runner who already has experience running at the elementary school level, Khan said, he could be turned into a top-caliber runner by the time he is a sophomore.

"We have had a hard time because the big schools that get further [in the state series] have a head start," Khan said. "The freshmen have run through grade school. But in the city, we've had to develop our kids."

Dale DeVinney, Mather's boys cross-country and track

coach, said there also has to be a change in the kids' mentality of what sport could take them further in life.

"For boys in the city, we have to get it in their heads that they might not be the next Michael Jordan," DeVinney said. "I'd love to be fed kids who have run track and cross-country [before high school], but I don't blame elementary school coaches."

Automatic bid still an issue

The issue of the Public League giving up its automatic bid to the state series in each sport still comes up, even though it has been four academic years since the change was made.

Boys basketball this season seemed to illustrate CPS chief executive officer Arne Duncan's intent when he made the change for the 2002-03 school year. Simeon and Marshall each brought home state trophies, with Simeon winning the Class AA title and Marshall finishing third.

"We felt those two teams were the two best in the state tournament," Davis said.

In girls basketball, Young went Downstate and finished third in the girls Class AA tournament for the second consecutive year.

"There are those who say the city championship is diminished because it doesn't have the automatic bid attached," Davis said. "Any time you win the championship in the largest local league in the state, it is very meaningful. Also, the historical significance has a great deal of value in itself. It is an elite list. Bragging rights go along with the title."

Davis stressed that every school gets another chance at the postseason when the city tournaments are over in each sport, unlike the days of the automatic bid. But he said there is still opposition to not having the bid.

"The decision was made before I came on as director," Davis said. "There are coaches who are against it. But I've come to grips with accepting the risk that comes with the elimination of the automatic bid, and there's always the chance you'll get no one [advancing to state]."

Another change announced this year will affect Public League schools in 2007. When the Illinois High School Association expands to four classes in boys and girls basketball, volleyball, baseball and softball and to three classes in boys golf and boys and girls track, there will be even more opportunities for Public League programs to go deep into the state playoffs.

"As they go to multiple classes, you'll see smaller-class

CPS basketball teams compete for a state title," Davis said. "Hope would fall in a different class than Young, and it would separate some of those schools who would normally be together [in a sectional complex].

"Before, we had one opportunity [with the automatic bid]. With [Class] A and AA, we have two. And then we'll have four.".

GOOD PUB

Calvin Davis ranks his five favorite things to watch during the 2005-2006 Public League Season:

- Derrick Rose hits the game winning shot in overtime of the Class AA boys basketball state championship game as Simeon beat Peoria Richwoods 31-29 for the 2006 state championship.

- Morgan Park goes overtime to win the Prep Bowl 14-13 against Brother Rice Mustangs big 3(Chris James, Ramone Johnson, and Demetrius Jones) shine.

- Morgan Park quarterback Demetrius Jones throws the game winning touchdown pass as time expires to win the city championship game. Jones signs with Notre Dame.

- Soccer star Jackie Vera shows off her shooting and dribbling skills all season for Lane Tech and leads the Indians to the Public League title.

- Three sport star Sherron Collins excels at football, basketball, and baseball for Crane, while Marshall's Patrick Beverley never tires while hooping it up.

DAVIS' LASTING MEMORY of 2006: Marshall girls basketball coach **Dorothy Gaters wins her 827th game,** the most in Illinois high school basketball history.

Printed in the United States
141252LV00002B/138/A